Lunchroom Theology is the
tives, Heather Gorman a
people have divided through discord and exclusion. But there's a better way to
live! Following the clear-cut example of Jesus, Gorman and Nelson provide a
path to a more loving, inclusive church—one that welcomes the outsider and
draws people together. This book is essential reading for anyone who is ready
to be part of a movement that unites people in our fractured times.

Dave Ferguson, author, *Hero Maker* and *B.L.E.S.S.*

By appealing to a fresh metaphor—the school lunchroom—Gorman and
Nelson invite us to bold, generative thinking about the human community.
In the typical lunchroom, there are all kinds of cliques and special interest
groups. The work of faith is to push all the tables together so that all may eat
together. These authors know about the sinister forces of fear, greed, and
violence that keep pushing the tables apart so that the work of one single
table is an ongoing, endless task. Amid this powerful imagery, these authors
provide compelling commentary on the Acts of the Apostles as the work
of one table. They show how the early church community was preoccupied
with "one table." This is a most suggestive read whose authors are alert to
various cultural clues and connections. We are invited to enlist in the good
work of the church, not unlike the work of reorganizing the lunchroom. We
will eat better when we all eat together!

Walter Brueggemann, Columbia Theological Seminary

We live in a fractured world where too many people not only disagree with
each other but actually despise each other. That's why this book is a balm,
like a cold drink on a hot summer day. Recently, I saw a poll that revealed
a disturbing number of both conservatives and liberals in America believe
their political opponents are not just wrong but evil. That's a hard world
to live in, especially for those of us who want to transcend worldly division and be "light in the darkness." Even in the church, we have over 35,000
Christian denominations, and have literally killed each other over doctrinal
differences ... despite Jesus' longest recorded prayer for us to be one as God
is one. And yet, it is clear that there is a version of "unity" that is shallow

and cheap and counterfeit … more concerned about the absence of tension than the presence of justice, as Martin Luther King, Jr. put it in his "Letter From Birmingham Jail." This book is not about that kind of cheap unity or shallow reconciliation. This book is not a *kumbaya*, feel-good, hug-some-body-you-disagree-with and "let's all just get along" kind of book. This book is an invitation to do something courageous—to listen, lean in, stay curious, and practice humility, especially with someone different from you. One of the most Spirit-quenching forces in the world is self-righteousness, and self-righteousness comes in many different forms but always essentially has the same posture of moral superiority that says, "Thank God that I am not like *those* people." Jesus shows us another way, a path forward beyond the polarized division of the world around us. He continually includes the excluded and challenges the chosen; he brings people together around a common table and shows us all how to be more loving, more just, more compassionate—that's what *Lunchroom Theology* is all about. I am convinced that one of the most radical things Jesus did was eat with all the wrong people. He had tax collectors and zealots sitting side by side, Pharisees and marginalized women becoming unlikely friends. The way of Jesus is scandalous—it was scandalous two thousand years ago and is still scandalous today. After all, it takes humility to believe that we are all equally sinful and equally sacred. So, read this book, and then join Jesus in eating with all the wrong people. Be a practitioner of lunchroom theology.

Shane Claiborne, author; activist; founder, Red Letter Christians

We're all tired of the small story of polarization that has become too common in our communities and families. We need a radical shift in our imaginations, a stretching of our sense of comfort. This wonderful work offers a hopeful way forward, calling us to something better—no less than the transformative, reconciling work of Jesus.

Mandy Smith, pastor; author; TheWayisTheWay.org

In *Lunchroom Theology*, Gorman and Nelson skillfully blend theology, ecclesiology, and missiology using the school lunchroom as a primary metaphor. This very approachable book invites us to reconceive gospel hospitality, offering a vision that can contribute to healing our fractured world. Resonating deeply with biblical principles, it is both accessible and inspirational. Highly recommended!

Debra Hirsch and Alan Hirsch, authors of numerous
books on missional discipleship, spirituality, and organization; founders,
the Forge Mission Training Network

Even people who are not great at math, like me, are good at division. We slice and sort nearly everyone into categories of people. We find "our group" and identify who is in and who is out. This is the way we save our brains and bodies calories. In doing so, we divide the world. Yet Jesus came to bring the world together, to free us from our silos and embrace "one another." Spanning the theological and political spectrum, Heather Gorman and Mark Nelson reveal to the church a better way forward. Here we find an accessible tool to the Jesus who turns over our tables in order that we may all sit together at his.

Sean Palmer, teaching pastor, Ecclesia, Houston;
author, *Unarmed Empire* and *Speaking By the Numbers*

Heather Gorman and Mark Nelson seem to actually believe that the practice of radical hospitality is at the heart of Christian community and that the table should be a forum for people of goodwill to share vastly different views and still break bread together. More than anything, I really hope they're right. *Lunchroom Theology* is a winsome rallying cry for wise, humble, Spirit-inspired Christian conversation. I thoroughly enjoyed reading it.

Michael Frost, Morling College, Sydney

"Everyone knows that in the lunchroom, it's all about the table." In *Lunchroom Theology*, Gorman and Nelson propose the high school lunchroom as an apt metaphor for the polarized world in which we live—a world complicated by issues of belonging, identity, and allegiance. The authors bring solid biblical scholarship into dialogue with examples from ancient history and contemporary popular culture to explore solutions to our brokenness, disconnection, and alienation. The result is a must read—a refreshing and winsomely written plea for unity and empathy, following Jesus' countercultural example to "push the tables together!"

In today's fractured world, the one missing component is thoughtfulness. *Lunchroom Theology* finally brings a metaphor, an explanation, and an option for Jesus-followers to live out our primary, collective job description in the world: to be reconcilers, bringing people together and then bringing them to God. Gorman and Nelson speak sensitively and clearly. This should be a must-read for any true disciple or discipler.

Given the way cultural and political battles have sliced right through the heart of our churches, I'd love to put a copy of *Lunchroom Theology* in the hands of every believer. Let's be honest: We need fewer food fights! Full of both popular references and deep, rich biblical reflections (from Sarah and Hagar to Mephibosheth to the Gospels and beyond), Gorman and Nelson help us remember a way of true table fellowship where diversity is permitted—even expected—and a richer unity is cherished because of the gospel.

Against forces that pull us apart along innumerable fault lines, Gorman and Nelson combine crisp writing, cultural resonance, scholarly research, and biblical grounding to invite us to push our divided lunchroom tables together, so we can imagine and embody a bigger "we" rooted in love, justice, and belonging.

The question of missiology is perhaps the most pressing of our moment. How ought Christians to witness in the divided states of America? Do we fight the culture wars? Do we elect a political strongman? Do we burn down the republic? Do we retreat into neomonastic communities? Do we update orthodoxy? Gorman and Nelson offer a fresh take on mission through the metaphor of a high school lunchroom. They argue our greatest apologetic is as dependent on our tables as our truth … creative, courageous, calculated, cross-shaped tables.

Tyler McKenzie, lead pastor, Northeast Christian Church
(Love the Ville' Church); podcast coproducer, *The Preacher and The Piano Man*; column writer, *Christian Standard*

Lunchroom Theology

Heather M. Gorman
& Mark Nelson

Lunchroom Theology

Pushing Tables Together in a Fractured World

100 MOVEMENTS
PUBLISHING

First published in 2024 by 100 Movements Publishing
www.100Mpublishing.com
Copyright © 2024 by Heather M. Gorman and Mark Nelson

Library of Congress Control Number: 2024911694

ISBN 978-1-955142-55-7 (print)
ISBN 978-1-955142-56-4 (eBook)

Cover design and interior design by Jude May
Image © leremy | iStock

100 Movements Publishing
An imprint of Movement Leaders Collective
Richmond, Virginia
www.movementleaderscollective.com

Heather
For Jamey, Anna, and Elise—you are my joy.

Mark
For my family—Michael, Hillary, Matthew, Carlyn, Meghan Marie, Porter June, and more to come—may you always choose the more beautiful way.

Heather and Mark
For Crossings, the faith community that continues to give us hope that a better way of following Jesus is possible.

Contents

Walking in Shoes
Too Small

If you don't like the road you're walking, start paving another one.
DOLLY PARTON

*The world changes according to the way people see it, and if you alter,
even by a millimeter, the way people look at reality, then you can change it.*
JAMES BALDWIN

Is it possible our world is just one big high school lunchroom?

It's likely the above sentence evokes a flood of images from your teenage years—some pleasant, many not so pleasant. For some, the grainy remembrance of a horribly fluorescent-lit, tile-floored cafeteria with a water-stained ceiling conjures up vivid reflections of the "good old days." For others, the recollection of those four arduous and painstaking years of adolescent dining will send them spiraling into multiple layers of misery. We begin this book with the assumption that most readers can identify with the reality of the high school lunchroom where every student learns how the world works in the twenty-three allotted minutes they have to secure a seat and wolf down a slice of rectangle pizza, slimy canned peaches, and a small carton of surprisingly delicious chocolate milk.

The high school lunchroom (or the "inner circle of hell" as some call it) is an integral slice of an American teenager's life.* It's the place where hormonally charged adolescents seek belonging and safety, where they form identity and long to be loved by someone … anyone. Writer Anne Lamott describes it like this:

> Here is the main thing I know about school lunches … it only *looked* like a bunch of kids eating lunch. It was really about opening our insides in front of everyone…. It was a precursor of the showers in … gym [class], where everyone could see your everything or your lack of everything, and smell the inside smells of your body, and the whole time you just knew you were going to catch something.[1]

There are few things in life as stressful as completing the journey through the lunch line on the first day of school and emerging into the vastness of the lunchroom holding your pale pink plastic tray divided into six small segments filled with culinary abominations while quickly scanning the room to survey the social landscape. *Where will I sit? Is there space for me at that table? Which table will be the safest? Is it worth the risk to approach that side of the cafeteria? If I choose poorly, will I be sentenced to remain at that table till I graduate? Why is everyone staring at me?*

Everyone knows that in the lunchroom, it's *all about the table.* Those aforementioned desires for belonging, identity, and safety, as well as your place in the social hierarchy, are quickly defined by your lunchroom table.

---

* Two important notes about the lunchroom metaphor for non-US readers: 1) In some ways, the levels and causes of polarization ("divided tables") vary from country to country. We acknowledge this, but as lifelong residents of the US, our perspective on these divisions is shaped by our national context, where they are currently particularly acute. However, we believe this metaphor applies in so many places beyond the US and trust that you—our insightful readers—can apply the metaphor in your own context. 2) We apologize if our examples of lunchroom staples (Lunchables, etc.) don't always translate in different cultures. We especially lament that many lunchrooms outside the US do not get to enjoy the delicacy of tater tots, which may be one of the few positive things to come out of a US lunchroom.

All students, teachers, and, yes, even the janitors (especially the janitors) know that the ecosystem of lunchroom tables can be complicated.

In the 2004 movie *Mean Girls*, social outcast Janis unfolds a detailed drawing of her school's lunchroom as she describes this ecosystem to the new girl, Cady:

> Now where you sit in the cafeteria is crucial because you've got everyone there. You've got your freshmen, ROTC Guys, preps, JV jocks, Asian nerds, cool Asians, varsity jocks, unfriendly Black hotties, girls who eat their feelings, girls who don't eat anything, desperate wannabes, burnouts, sexually active band geeks, the greatest people you will ever meet, *and* the worst: beware of The Plastics.[2]

Add to the list as you will—soccer boys, thespians, partiers, hippies, anime lovers, artsy people, nice and nerdy seniors, the lax bros, the popular sophomores, and the *almost* popular juniors. The list can be endless.

Nearly every American teen movie has illustrated how the world works in a high school lunchroom—from *Grease* to *Superbad* to *Can't Buy Me Love*. And, according to the 2006 cinematic classic *High School Musical*, there's one cardinal rule: "Don't mess with the flow." Apparently, staying cool in the lunchroom hierarchy means sticking to the status quo—the balance of the lunchroom universe should *never* be tampered with.[3]

At a *much* deeper sociological level, psychologist and educator Beverly Daniel Tatum, in her book *Why Are All the Black Kids Sitting Together in the Cafeteria*, categorizes the ecosystem of a lunchroom as "the search for personal identity that intensifies in adolescence." She believes it involves "several dimensions of a teenager's life: vocational plans, religious beliefs, values and preferences, political affiliations and beliefs, gender roles, and ethnic identities."[4]

Unfortunately, as ridiculous as it might sound, we believe the lunchroom closely resembles the world into which every one of us graduates. The most frightening part is that the divisions we endure in high school will likely be the least severe and least damaging we'll experience in our lives. Those petri dishes of angst-filled, status-seeking, afraid-of-their-own-shadow teenagers sorting through relationships and social dynamics are just a foretaste of what is to come. In the real world, our divisions may be less hormonally fueled and seemingly more "sophisticated," but they are still there—and the hurt and separation run deep.

So, then, in response to our original question, we propose the answer is yes. Yes, our world really is just one gigantic high school lunchroom, segregated by its self-sustaining hierarchy and adolescent loathing of "the other." In the coming pages, we'll unpack why we believe this to be the case and why we think society is full of adults searching for most of the same things they've been longing for since they first washed down a grilled cheese with a swig of Capri Sun on their way to freshmen algebra. And the results are the same, just adult-sized—we find ourselves as a culture sitting around a multitude of different tables, each with people who often only care about *their* table and who would do anything to keep the status quo, to keep their influence, status, and power, even at the cost of hurting others. And yes, as we hope you would agree, this way of living in the world is freakishly broken.

And no, it is *not* the way of Jesus.

A Better Way to Live in the Lunchroom

We believe the way of Jesus entails resisting a world where we remain separate at each of our own tables, divided according to skin color, political beliefs, theological stances, denominational alignment, geography, or whatever other categories might exist—and there are *so* many categories. We are convinced that Jesus' vision for the lunchroom is utterly incompatible with the way we have defaulted to sorting each other in our world. And so, alternatively, and perhaps subversively, we believe the way of Jesus, and thus also the way of Jesus' followers, is one where we push all the tables together and where we are each commissioned to invite everyone, including every "other," to that table—even those we would have never considered sitting with in high school (perhaps especially them!).

We do need to clarify one thing before we go any further: The premise of this book is that our *world* is a giant high school lunchroom. The *church* is *not* the lunchroom. The church does not own or control the lunchroom.

The church has a presence in the lunchroom; it is impacted by the culture and dynamics and "rules" of the lunchroom; it has some of its own rules and bullies and cool kids and gatekeepers; it has different tables in different corners of the lunchroom. But the lunchroom is much, much bigger than the church.

And yet, as the church, pushing tables together needs to start with us in an effort to manifest and embody the prayer of Jesus in John 17:21: "Father, may they all be one as You are in Me and I am in You; may they be in Us, for by this unity the world will believe that You sent Me" (VOICE). If Jesus meant what he said in John 17, then there is urgent and consequential work to do with extremely high stakes. Unless, of course, we enjoy being stuck in an infinite loop of adolescent thinking and behavior.

There is a better way for us to live in this lunchroom if we're willing to push tables together. We believe this is what Jesus had in mind when he embodied a different kind of lunchroom theology—a theology that welcomed all to the table, insisted that every person had inherent value, and subverted the established social hierarchies of his day. This is what the New Testament writers incessantly called for as well. In passages like Galatians 3:28—"There is no longer Jew or Greek; there is no longer slave or free; there is no longer male and female, for all of you are one in Christ Jesus"—Paul is admonishing the church to call the entire lunchroom culture of the day into question. He is insisting that if this Jesus is indeed risen from the dead, then the entire lunchroom needs to be reorganized. And in this new reality brought about by the work of Jesus, every person in every category is of equal value. Everybody.

Throughout this book, we want to invite you into the lunchroom theology of Jesus and of those first followers living in the wake of his resurrection, in the hope that we might all begin to form a better lunchroom theology of our own. But before you read any further, we want to address a few important questions.

Should You Keep Reading?

Like most authors, we've spent a lot of time thinking about who we're writing to. You have our word that we've done our due diligence in attempting to understand the multiplicity of angles our readers may be coming from.

To be as transparent as possible, we want you to know that we are writing to

... those of you who feel that over the last decade or two, because of rising hate and vitriol, your table has gotten significantly smaller, bringing with it an overwhelming sense of hopelessness or grief.

... those of you who sometimes feel you have no home—no table at which to sit. None of the labels that so many insist on applying (evangelical, progressive, conservative, liberal, fundamentalist) really fit.

... those of you who find yourself on *both* sides of the aisle, while those most influential in the lunchroom ecosystem try to force everyone to choose a side and settle at their clearly labeled table.

... those of you who have a suffocating weight on your chest as you realize that the hatred and discord run deeper than you initially thought.

... those of you who prefer to choose your faith community based on a biblical Christology and missiology as opposed to an "ology" or belief system based upon anything else.

... those of you who want to continue to learn, grow, discuss, and resist the temptation of settling into the camp of "I know all there is to know."

... those of you who are seeking to pursue the radical ways of Jesus in community, in hopes of one day, once again, eating Thanksgiving dinner with your family without teetering oh so close to fisticuffs.

... those of you who want to sit around one table, a table with Jesus at the center, and who want to change the conversation.

... those of you who long to play your part in the restoration of all things instead of feeling paralyzed by the grief, sadness, and fear of the current lunchroom, which resembles so little of Jesus.

If you see yourself in any of "those," we'd love for you to keep reading.

May We Disturb Your Peace?

If you decide to keep reading, please understand we're inviting you to live in some tension—not tension with one another (there's plenty of that already), but the tension that naturally arises when we're no longer willing to tolerate the current state of the lunchroom. Author and activist James Baldwin describes how a writer brings out this tension. He says, "A writer is, by definition, a disturber of the peace."[5] Disturbing one another's peace is refusing to allow the status quo to remain. In that sense, we hope to "disturb your peace," to disrupt whatever might need to be disrupted, to expose our current lunchroom as the antithesis to Jesus' vision for the lunchroom.

In all of this, we don't expect that you'll agree with everything in this book. We expect that you may have issues with some of what we write. But we also hope that in the midst of that tension and disagreement, you might have the courage to consider a different way that works to heal the brokenness and dysfunction of the current lunchroom. We're not seeking uniformity in ideas and beliefs, but we are asking you to come together to pursue unity, the kind of unity for which Jesus prayed. As author and missiologist Ed Stetzer writes,

> Unity doesn't require uniformity. We can be tightly bonded together in love and still retain our distinctions. In a world which is becoming increasingly polarized over ideological issues, the Church's ability to hold deeply held differences together with unity is a witness of the power of the gospel. It is also a model for the world to follow.[6]

Entering into that tension doesn't require us to suspend our deeply held convictions, nor discard our doctrinal differences in the pursuit of identical beliefs. "Instead," Stetzer continues, "it means that we approach the ecumenical table looking to identify *where we can* work together rather than looking for reasons *why we can't.*"[7]

Of course, it would be much easier to remain at each of our own tables, hoping things will just work out in the end. And we realize the work can feel too hard and uncomfortable for some, especially when it involves sitting with people we disagree with and attempting to wrestle with the sacred text of the Bible. Pastor and writer John Pavlovitz explains the risk:

> Once it begins in earnest, it's terrifying, which is why so many Christians are content never looking at the Bible too closely or challenging a

theological precept too forcefully—not because we don't feel such things are needed, but because we're afraid of the path they might lead us down. It's just easier and less taxing to take a pastor's word for it and act as though we're fine with that, operating on a sort of existential autopilot that stays safely in the superficial.[8]

Disturbing the peace means we might be uncomfortable with who else is at the table and what Scripture reveals if we start looking at it more closely. In this book, we engage *everyone* in this wrestling, and in doing so, we quote authors and teachers you may not like, inviting people from *other* tables to join our table. That's why the above paragraphs quote both Ed Stetzer *and* John Pavlovitz, two authors who land at quite different places on many important theological issues. Citation of a person's work doesn't mean endorsement of all their ideas. Rather, it's part of what it means to invite different approaches and perspectives to a discussion around one table while pursuing the way of Jesus. It's learning to live in the tension and to ask and grapple with the questions that we don't know how to face and that have kept us at separate tables for far too long.

Curating the Story

As we enter into this conversation, we think it's important to be conscious of the fact that most who decide to journey through these pages will do so with varied approaches to Scripture. This is of obvious relevance as we consider pushing our tables together. To pretend that we all view Scripture from the same perspective is a bit simplistic and naive. We all approach Scripture with different hermeneutical lenses (methods or theories of interpretation), and to deny that is, within itself, a hermeneutical lens.

So, before we go any further, let us be as clear as we possibly can about a foundational tenet in our approach to Scripture. We believe this divinely inspired text that has guided, empowered, confused, and spoken personally and intimately to so many of us functions best as a plowshare. The plowshare is the main cutting blade of a plow, which tills and cultivates the soil so that it might be ready to produce an abundance of whatever seed is planted and which cuts through both the soft and ready-to-be-planted soil as well as the hard and fallow ground that might take a bit more effort to prepare for growth. We believe that process describes well what the Holy Scriptures do for us. They cultivate in us a place where the truth that is revealed can be planted in us, the soil, allowing for new life to come forth. A good lunchroom theology approaches the Word of God not with the intent to cut down and destroy life but to reveal, plant, and grow us as God's beloved creation.

Scripture is inviting us into a story—a narrative that, from beginning to end, is one of God putting his family back together. As the late author and theologian Frederick Buechner writes,

> For all its vast diversity and unevenness, it is a book with a plot and a plot that can be readily stated. God makes the world in love. For one reason or another the world chooses to reject God. God will not reject the world but continues his mysterious and relentless pursuit of it to the end of time.[9]

God calls us to understand our individual stories in light of his larger story, and he calls us to participate in his mission of reconciliation and restoration.

We want to acknowledge that we all bring baggage into our discussions of Scripture. At one time or another, we all have fallen into the tendency of managing and controlling, dividing up and handing out, of curating Scripture to only support an already established belief or doctrine. But such tendencies unfortunately increase our fractures rather than heal them. The sad reality is that all of us—whether as individuals, churches, organizations, or denominations—are guilty of curating the text with only *our* table in mind. The response, of course, shouldn't be to abandon Scripture but rather to curate it *well*. We believe that when we do curate it well (and we know none of us will ever do this perfectly), the story can change us and the lunchroom.

Because we believe the lunchroom in Jesus' time was not unlike today's, we will lean heavily on the narratives of both Jesus and his early followers as they attempted to embody and incarnate these ways of Jesus in the earliest expressions of the church. We believe that if we enter these stories as our own, rather than as relics of the past, they can profoundly change us. This transformation can empower us, as Jesus followers, to rethink how we might begin to push the tables together in our fractured world.

Who Are We to Guide This Conversation?

Besides the fact that we each possess our own lunchroom scars, both from our actual high school days and from living in these extraordinarily divided times, our approach to this topic comes with years of experience and even more so from an insatiable desire to learn a new way to be the church in this fractured world. So, before we go any further, we want to give you a little background on who we are and why we're writing this book together.

Growing up in the church has given me (Mark) quite a few different perspectives on the tables of which we speak. When I say "growing up in the church," this includes playing the infant Jesus at our small-town church's Christmas pageant as my mom and dad wore the appropriate dramatic bathrobes to play Mary and Joseph. When you think about it, the Savior of the world is quite a heavy role to lay on a three-month-old.

Over the last six decades, I have inherited a faith in a God who loves me unconditionally from a family who loves me deeply. The foundational narrative I received growing up in faith and the church is a gift that I am forever grateful for. However, I have also found myself intertwined in more than a few false narratives along the way. The ecclesial narrative I was immersed in included a baseline understanding that we were the *only* ones that had it right; we were *the* church to provide all the right answers to all of life's questions; there were those who were in and those who were out. This narrative bred a belief that, even if there were multiple tables in the lunchroom, we were obviously at the right one, and those other tables should be avoided and feared. As a result, I excelled at excluding others based upon spoken and unspoken qualifiers.

In something that was more caught than taught, I had settled into a belief in God that was strictly limited to my own understanding and experiences. This kind of small-minded approach to the divine formed in me a narrow, fear-driven, reductionist faith. It was the kind of theology that all but eliminated the possibility of pushing the tables together in the way of Jesus. My story for so many years was therefore a story of very small exclusionary tables because, quite honestly, my God was way too small and exclusionary.

Let me be clear: I do not place the blame for this understanding of God anywhere except upon myself. I have to take responsibility, regardless of outside experiences and influences, and own that this tiny lunchroom table at which I have sat for much of my life was, in so many ways, of my own making. I do not believe this small-minded table was predicated on hate or a sense of self-superiority but simply the natural result of a life lived primarily among people who talked, thought, believed, and acted exactly as I did. It meant my lunchroom table was small and set off in some faraway corner of the lunchroom, and I had little, if any, understanding of those sitting elsewhere.

Working in multiple expressions of vocational ministry (youth, university, and local church ministries) over the last three decades has enabled me to see, appreciate, and understand a variety of perspectives. As a result, I have attempted to practice a deeper and more expansive lunchroom theology. This has been expressed in two key spheres.

First, in 2007, I led the planting of a church in the city center of Knoxville, Tennessee.[10] Since then, our faith community has sought to follow in the radical ways of Jesus by crafting an expression of church that provides a space for any and every person from any and every corner in the lunchroom to scoot themselves up to the table. Though far from perfect, together we've wrestled with questions of faith and life while partaking in the liberation and restoration that we believe Jesus offers.

Second, I lead a collaboration throughout our city that fosters learning communities among churches of all shapes, colors, and sizes. We attempt to set aside all our lunchroom tendencies and instead pursue kingdom-of-God things together in our area.[11] This current calling is propelled by a passion for us to be one in the way Jesus desires for his church.

I (Heather) will never forget the time my husband and I met the realtor who sold us our first house. We were driving around Waco, Texas, looking for a house we could afford on two graduate student stipends. When our realtor's husband, who joined us that day, found out we were both doing

PhDs in religion, he asked what denomination we were a part of. In other words, which church table did we sit at, and did we play nice with those at his church table?

I hate that question about denominations. Not because it's a bad question but because I come from a religious tradition that makes answering that question tricky. My tradition was birthed in response to denominational divisions, and our founders tried to start a movement that would bring unity to this division. They didn't want people to have to sign off on a creed to be a part of their church. "No creed but Christ," they said. "No book but the Bible." And so they rejected denominational hierarchies that tried to ensure uniformity. They refused denominational labels and instead said, "We're Christians only (though not the only Christians!)." I love so much of the spirit of this movement, but it made answering the question "What denomination are you from?" really hard. I wasn't Baptist or Lutheran or Methodist or Episcopalian. Our churches, for the most part, rejected the labels. Christ was, at least in theory, our uniter.

But answering "Christian" didn't help my realtor's husband know which lunch table I sat at. I went with our group's more common title in the south—hoping we'd get back to mortgage rates and renovation potential. My plan failed.

His response: "Oh, the churches who think they're the only ones who are saved."

Awkward silence.

He wasn't totally wrong. There are many from my tradition who have made such exclusive thinking a key part of their identity.[12] The irony that a movement founded on unity became so known for its divisiveness is not lost on me. And this is probably where I should confess that I participated in that divisiveness. I remember spending hours on the phone when I was a teenager, trying to convince my friends from the "denominations" to be baptized in the same way I was because I was certain their baptism—done in a different way or for a different reason—was invalid, and thus they were going to hell. I was terrified for them. And although I believe my motives were good, those motives were entangled with a prideful belief that I was the captain of God's lunch table. And as the self-appointed captain of the table, my job was to recruit people to my table, screen who was allowed to sit there, and then make sure that everyone at my table knew how wrong the other tables were.

Not all folks in my tradition believe what my realtor's husband or my fourteen-year-old self did, but, as is true for all of us, my background shaped me both positively and negatively. Although there are parts of my heritage that aren't perfect, its commitment to Scripture, the church, and gathering around the table are all values I bring to this book. My hope is that my life experience, alongside my study of Scripture and church history, have given me a broader and more charitable view of the lunchroom and—perhaps most importantly—the humility to know the lunchroom is Jesus', not mine.

Throughout my life, both in the church and in my vocation as a professor of the New Testament, I have remained committed to this tradition, at least in part because I think our founders were attempting to address the lunch-room problem. They lamented the divisions they saw in the church and thought those divisions got in the way of the church achieving Jesus' vision of bringing people to him. They took seriously Jesus' words in John 17:23, where Jesus prayed that his followers would "become completely one, so that the world may know that you have sent me and have loved them even as you have loved me." They believed that becoming one, somehow pushing together the lunch tables and learning to work together, was how the world would come to know God's love and who Jesus is. In many ways, that vision is the vision of this book.

Our experiences share some common threads: Both of us were raised in the same religious tradition and have spent our lives committed to the churches and universities of this tradition. Over the last decade, we've shared many of the same tables, both literally and metaphorically. And yet in many ways our stories are different. We are female and male, Millennial and Baby Boomer, professor and pastor, PC user and Mac enthusiast. We don't see eye to eye on every issue, and our different ministry contexts have meant that our experiences of Scripture and the lunchroom have not always been the same.

In the midst of both these similarities and differences, we share a lament for this divided and fractured world. And we also share a hope that encountering the stories of Scripture and thinking deeply about how they intersect with our own world can help us envision a better way to live in the lunchroom.

A Theology of Clicks

We realize that the perspectives and experiences that each reader carries are as varied as the number of readers. And we know that some will want to move from *Mean Girls* to the radical ways of Jesus more quickly than others. The conversation changes at a different pace for every one of us. Some are ready to dive in headlong; others are just dipping their toes in. As authors, we expect that. All we are asking for is a little forward movement.

Think of it this way: Imagine a dial that contains the letters "A" to "Z," and imagine that each of us resides somewhere on that dial next to a specific letter and that the goal is always to be moving through the alphabet toward "Z." Some of you enter this book around "L," and you cannot wait to move toward "M" and further. Others come in around "C," and the most you hope for is to get to "D" or "E" (and if things get crazy maybe all the way to "F"). This process of learning has been called a theology of "clicks."[13] Each time you make a move or understand a new truth, it is a "click" forward. The point is not that some are more enlightened than others and get to "Z" more quickly, but rather that throughout history, including in Scripture, we see God connecting with people where they are and moving them closer to his original intent. God meets people in their cultural moment and draws them forward with a click or two. God is the one who turns the dial. In all of it, God is inviting us *forward*. All each of us needs is a willingness to move.

Ultimately, we are writing this book because we love Jesus and we love the church (in that order). And we have great faith and hope in both. We have hope that this divisive, sectarian, everyone-sits-at-their-own-table faith is not what the future holds for those who follow Jesus. It cannot be. We were made for more than this. Our theologies, Christologies, and eccle-siologies have shrunk to the point that they have very little resemblance to the way of living in the world that Jesus calls us to. As *New York Times* columnist David Brooks has said, "We all are walking in shoes too small for us."[14]

We hope this book plays some role in helping us see the larger story that God has called us into and provides a vision and vocabulary for how we might bring healing to this fractured lunchroom.

2

Assessing the Fracture

Someone told me in a moment of honesty, "I'm not sure we can be friends unless I know you hate the things I hate."
DAN WHITE JR.

It's time we decided to stop being afraid of each other.
NIKKI GIOVANNI

Whenever someone asks what this book is about, our first response is always the same: "Our world is one giant high school lunchroom." Without fail, people nod and agree, often with an uncomfortable and awkward laugh as they try *not* to remember their own high school lunchroom experiences. Most don't need further explanation—they just get it. They easily see how the lunchroom dynamics play out in their families, their workplaces, their neighborhoods, their churches, and their social media feeds. They've experienced its effects firsthand. We assume you have, too.

Of course, this book isn't just here to defend the premise that our world is a giant high school lunchroom. We're not here to simply point out problems; we want to challenge our readers (and ourselves) to stop settling for the current state of the lunchroom. Our larger goal is to show how the ways and teachings of Jesus help those who follow him to envision and embody a better lunchroom. If the church does this—if it shows a better way of living in the lunchroom—we believe it has the potential to impact a watching world.

But to adequately address the problem, we must understand the problem, and not just at an anecdotal or gut level. Although most of us can articulate the effects of the lunchroom dynamic in our world, we have a harder time explaining how it got this way and an even harder time imagining how to remedy it. And like toddlers, who become overwhelmed with emotions when they don't have the words to describe them, one of two things happens: Either we *don't* try to understand what's going on (and so, at best, live in a state of perpetual frustration or, at worst, sink into despair)[1] or, if we *do* make the effort to understand the problem, we find ourselves resorting to overly simplistic explanations (social media, whatever cable news network I dislike, kids these days, Boomers) that fail to fully engage the complexity of the issue. Overly simplistic explanations are likely to result in equally simplistic solutions. To avoid this oversimplification, we're going to spend this chapter and the next trying to describe both the sociological and the theological origins of the lunchroom.

The Big Sort

What we're referring to as "the lunchroom phenomenon" is called "the big sort" by social commentator Bill Bishop. In his book by the same name, he tracks trends in where and why people have moved locations in the US since the mid-1970s. Bishop argues that, although there have always been migration trends, these trends have changed since the '70s because people began sorting themselves geographically by age, income, education, race, sexual orientation, and other factors. The result? "In 1976, less than a quarter of Americans lived in places where the presidential election was a landslide. By 2004, nearly half of all voters lived in landslide counties."[2] (A landslide county is a county where one party won by 20 percent or more.) In 2016, 80 percent of US counties had landslide victories for their preferred presidential candidate.[3] Though Bishop used election results as a measure, his findings weren't only—or even primarily—about politics. He explains, "The Big Sort, then, is not simply about political partisanship, about how Americans vote every couple of years. *It is a division in what they value, in how they worship, and in what they expect out of life* .... It is the way Americans have chosen to live, an unconscious decision to cluster in communities of like-mindedness."[4] Even though so many of us hated the high school lunchroom, Bishop's research details how we continue to divide into tables well after we hang up our graduation robes to collect dust in the hallway closet.

While the origins of the lunchroom dynamic predate the period Bishop studied (more on that in the next chapter), something exacerbated it in the 1970s. Bishop claims it was fueled by prosperity and economic security. In other words, increased financial means combined with the introduction of interstate highways, air transportation, widespread higher education, and laws enforcing racial equality enabled people to reorder their lives "around their values, their tastes, and their beliefs" in ways previous generations weren't able to.[5]

These shifts weren't just secular. Bishop found significant evidence that faith also accounted for migration choices. For example, people leaving counties with a high percentage of religious conservatives rarely moved to counties with a high percentage of political liberals.[6] People's religion impacted where they moved, and then where they moved impacted their faith.

His explanation of this dynamic is worth quoting in full:

> Churches grew more politically homogeneous ... and so did civic clubs, volunteer organizations, and, dramatically, political parties. People weren't simply moving. The whole society was changing. Prosperity had altered what people wanted out of life and what they expected from their government, their churches, and their neighborhoods. The Big Sort was big because it constituted a social and economic reordering around values, ways of life, and communities of interest.[7]

He adds later that people no longer "have to live with neighbors or community groups that might force them to compromise their principles or their tastes."[8] Think about that idea for a moment. Is being unwilling to be *neighbors* with someone with different principles and tastes *really* what Jesus intended? Jesus' response to a lawyer who asked him to define his neighbor suggests it's not (Luke 10:25–37). But we're getting ahead of ourselves.

The Law of Group Polarization

Bishop's findings are even more significant in light of what Harvard Law professor Cass Sunstein calls "the law of group polarization." The law of group polarization shows that when people or groups of similar beliefs come together, they become more extreme.[9] Regardless of the topic—gun rights, raising the minimum wage, environmental issues, or any other divisive subject—when individuals discuss these topics with like-minded people, it reinforces their existing beliefs and makes them more extreme. In another study, Sunstein and Reid Hastie observed this same dynamic occurring in various contexts—groups deliberating on political issues, groups considering risky behavior, and groups assessing other groups.[10] The liberals became more liberal when deliberating with other liberals. The same went for conservatives. People who were only *considering* risky behavior were more willing to actually *engage in* risky behavior after spending time with others who engaged in such behavior. The reverse was true for those who were risk averse—they became less likely to engage in risky behavior after spending time with others who didn't usually engage in such behavior. The groups and the individuals within them grew more extreme.

Deliberation with like-minded folks also increased consensus among the groups. While there was some diversity in opinion prior to the discussions, that variation became less frequent after deliberating with people of a similar mindset.[11] Sunstein explains two dynamics underlying this pattern—"social influences on behavior" and "limited argument pools."[12] We'll use iPhone users as a low-stakes example to show these dynamics. The first dynamic, "social influences on behavior," is the notion that we want other group members to view us favorably, and challenging the dominant view may put that favor at risk, so we don't. If I'm gathered with a bunch of iPhone users and want to maintain good standing with this group, I'm less likely to point out that my friend's Android phone takes better pictures than my iPhone because I don't want to risk alienation in this Apple-loving group. The second dynamic, "limited argument pools," is the idea that if a group is comprised primarily of individuals with a similar belief, their arguments are going to be weighted in favor of that belief. People at the "iPhone users" table are going to have more reasons why iPhones are good but fewer about the quality of Androids, which is going to confirm their initial beliefs about iPhones being better. Their argument pool is limited.

The power of groups is that sometimes people will choose loyalty to their group or maintaining good standing in their group *over truthfulness.* The German author Bastian Berbner, in his book *In Search of Common Ground,* tells of an experiment in 1951 by the social psychologist Solomon Asch where participants were shown a piece of paper with a line on it. Next, they were given a paper with three lines of differing lengths on it and asked to identify the line that matched the one on the first piece of paper—a very easy task that more than 99 percent could achieve. Berbner explains what happened next:

> Then Asch altered the experiment. He introduced six extra people into the room who—unbeknownst to the participant—were part of the experiment setup. The examiner first asked the six new people in the room, one after the other, which line was the same length as the first one. Because they were in on it, all six gave the same—wrong—answer. The actual participant was asked last. In 37 percent of cases, the participant also gave the wrong answer, even though they must have known perfectly well that it wasn't true. *They opted for loyalty to the group over truthfulness.*[13]

All of this reveals just how strong group dynamics at the lunch table can be. Asch's research shows that fear of losing a seat at the table can mean that even truth takes a back seat.

So, to summarize the sociological perspective thus far in this chapter: We have the big sort—Americans are clustering with others who are like-minded. And we have the law of group polarization—when like-minded individuals cluster they become more extreme. And, at times, a person's desire to maintain good standing at their table will even lead them to prioritize group loyalty over truthfulness. Is this a recipe worse than the tuna noodle casserole the lunch ladies cooked up in the early '90s? Political commentator David French thinks so. He connects the big sort to the law of group polarization and concludes, "Put those two things together, and you

have two groups radicalizing without realizing it, then standing—mouths
agape—at their radicalizing opposition and wondering, 'What happened to
them?' The answer is clear: *The same thing that's happening to you*."[14]

Oof.

Manifestations of the Sort

We believe that these two phenomena—the big sort and the law of group
polarization—explain so much of what we're witnessing day after day in our
communities: anger, loneliness, fear, hate, distrust, and the like. Researcher
and author Brené Brown, reflecting on Bishop's work, puts it another way:
"This sorting leads us to make assumptions about the people around us,
which in turn fuels disconnection."[15]

Disconnection. We think that's the best word, at least in sociological
terms, for the umbrella under which all of the manifestations of the big
sort fall. These communal fractures—those mentioned above, along with
violence, blame, objectification, disgust—they're all expressions of disconnection. And they are telltale signs that we're in a very broken and fractured
lunchroom. The works of Bishop, Sunstein, and Brown don't just describe
how we got here sociologically; they also show us that our attempt at fixing
this disconnection—by grouping with people who are like us and thus who
are presumably harder to hate—is actually exacerbating the problem by
making us more extreme, anxious, belligerent, and distrustful of others. For
the remainder of this chapter, we will explore the current causes and manifestations of this disconnection so that we can then reflect on how Jesus
shows us a better way.

Disconnection and Identity

The causes and manifestations of disconnection (and it's impossible to
distinguish what *causes* disconnection from what is *caused by* the disconnection) are often deeply attached to our sense of self. Sociologist Matthew
Vos explains how the tendency to separate from those we perceive to be
unlike us is a part of how we form identities. Vos uses the language of the
"stranger" to refer to those "who we work to distance ourselves from, often

in symbolic ways, not because they pose a danger to us but because our contrast with them—our superiority against their inferiority—affirms our dominant and desirable position in the social hierarchy."[16] He cites Jim Crow laws as a vivid example of this phenomenon. Jim Crow laws enforced racial segregation after the 1865 abolition of slavery, making any blurring of the lines between races a punishable offense. Jim Crow laws, Vos says, "all pretty much boil down to maintaining a well-defined out-group contrast that was favorable to White identity and that subordinated Black culture and identity."[17]

Creating and sustaining "in" groups and "out" groups happens all around us. We see it in education and parenting. Parents who send their kids to public school often understand themselves over and against those who homeschool and vice versa. Vos observes, "The mode of school you endorse … functions as an identity platform that serves to remind you of your own diligence and morality in the face of those who use other, 'lesser,' educational approaches with their children."[18] The same would apply to parents who stay at home with their young kids over and against those who send their kids to preschool or day care. I (Heather), who work outside the home full-time and whose kids both attended preschool, once had someone tell me, "Well I didn't send my kids to preschool because I didn't want someone other than me raising my kids." Someone else confessed that she assumed I looked down on her as a stay-at-home mom because she wasn't showing her kids that women have value in the workplace. Though both comments stung in different ways, they highlight how fear—in this case, the fear of parental inadequacy—can lead us to rank ourselves and others on various rungs of the social ladder. I think both comments were coming from places of insecurity—the perpetual fear that so many of us parents have that we're falling short. And so, to mask that fear, we try to affirm ourselves by moving higher on the social ladder and making ourselves look or feel superior to others.

This dynamic, of course, isn't limited to parenting or education. We see it in the choices people make about food, health care, or climate-related issues. Organic. Vegan. Paleo. Pro-vax. Anti-vax. Gas-fueled vehicle. Hybrid.

And boy oh boy, do we see it in religious denominations and theologies. Christians have been just as complicit in this disconnection. The churches birthed out of the Protestant Reformation were formed in protest against the Catholic church. A small town near us has two Baptist churches right across the street from one another—one the Providence Baptist Church, the other Crossroads Baptist. Did Crossroads Baptist split from Providence Baptist and passive-aggressively name their church to signify their new location? Or did Providence Baptist split from Crossroads Baptist and passive-aggressively name their church to signal God's preordained blessing for their formation? But it's not just within denominations. Egalitarians define themselves over and against complementarians, Reformed over and against Arminian, traditional views on sexuality over and against affirming ones, theistic evolutionists over and against young earth creationists. There is seemingly no end to the reasons Christians will sort themselves into separate lunch tables.

We are not saying that these groups or their positions or theologies don't matter. We absolutely believe that they do. Nor are we saying that we need to ignore these differences. Absolutely not. We are saying that the more we continue to group with only those who are like-minded and the more we continue to distance ourselves from those with whom we disagree, the worse off we become. When we sort into lunch tables based on all these identity labels, we understand one another less. We are more anxious. We are less connected. We are more extreme in our views. We become more certain, leaving less room for alternative perspectives.[19] We become defensive. We are suspicious of others. We get satisfaction in watching others fall. We crave belonging but fear we're not worthy of it.

The Three Ds of the Devil

My (Heather's) husband's family tells of an infamous sermon preached at their home church decades ago—"The Three Ds of the Devil." According to the preacher, the three Ds were *drinking*, *dancing*, and *divorce*. While others might rightly claim that my dance moves are indeed of the devil, I'll withhold judgment on this sermon since I didn't hear it. But as we researched disconnection, we discovered what could aptly be dubbed "The Three Ds of Disconnection"—*distance, distortion,* and *distrust.*

Simply stated, sitting at lunch tables with only people who are like us creates *distance* from those who are different. This distance, in turn, *distorts* our perception of others. And with a distorted view of others, we default to a much more extreme and radical perception of the other, which breeds a basic *distrust.* Distance breeds distortion, and distortion breeds distrust.

And if it's easier to distrust people from a distance, it's easier to hate them, too. This is the basis of Brené Brown's famous chapter, "People are Hard to Hate Close Up. Move In."[20] It's easy to hate a group of strangers, whose stories we don't know, whose hopes and hurts we haven't experienced. But when we zoom in, we recognize that the narratives we hear from a distance don't always hold up. For example, larger societal narratives might portray all gun owners as irresponsible and violence-obsessed, and we're sure some are. But when I (Heather) get up close to gun owners in my wider family, these caricatures are oversimplified. Instead, I see folks who cherish hunting as a part of their family tradition and even their connection to the land and their family. Hunting stray groundhogs is how they protect the crops on their family's land. And hunting deer is how they spend time in nature and bond with their kids, and then eat the haul of their sport all year long.

From a distance we can distort and distrust those who are different from us, but when we remove the first D (distance), the other two start to crumble. Brown challenges us with this question: "What if what we experience up close is real, and what we hear on the news and from the mouths of politicians who are jockeying for power needs to be questioned? It is not easy to hate people up close."[21]

Unfortunately, if left unchecked, these three Ds of disconnection can lead to a fourth—*dehumanization.* Philosopher Michelle Maiese defines dehumanization as "the process of demonizing the enemy, making them seem less than human and hence not worthy of humane treatment."[22] Brown explains how this process is connected to distortion and distrust: "Dehumanization often starts with creating an *enemy image.* As we take sides, lose trust, and get angrier and angrier, we not only solidify an idea of our enemy, but also start to lose our ability to listen, communicate, and practice even a modicum of empathy."[23] When the other side becomes not just morally inferior but dangerous, we can justify any number of attitudes or actions against them.

Take, for instance, driving a car. In an all too relatable routine, comedian George Carlin describes how there's something about being behind the wheel that makes us unreasonably angry at others: "Have you ever noticed that when you're driving, anyone who is driving slower than you is an idiot, and anyone driving faster than you is a maniac?" He then narrates a not-so-hypothetical speech we might make behind the wheel: "Look at this idiot here. Will you just *look* at this idiot just creeping along?" Then, pretending to see a car zooming past, he says, "Whoa! Look at that maniac go!"[24] The audience erupts in laughter because, well, we've all been there.

Under almost no circumstances would we call someone an idiot or a maniac to their face, but put ten feet and a window between us, and suddenly all bets are off. There is a *perceived* distance created, which leaps over distortion and distrust and lands us at dehumanization. Suddenly it's okay to believe that other drivers are brainless humans with no regard for anyone but themselves. For every driver that raises our ire, we write a story in our minds based on what they look like, what kind of car they drive, or how the cigarette hangs off their bottom lip as they unsuccessfully attempt to stay in their lane while texting. If the back of their truck is filled with trash, if they have a bumper sticker of a candidate or sports team we dislike, or if their personalized license plate is too hard to decipher, we immediately create labels for them and make our thoughts known, much to the chagrin of our passengers who wonder what in the world is happening to us.

And if the glass of a car window can so easily create the distance that leads us to dehumanize others, how much more the glass of a phone screen? Emboldened by the distance of the internet, void of body language or real-time emotional responses, family members make accusations against one another online that they would never make in person. Friends, acquaintances, and neighbors—some with deep, shared histories—call one another names and question each other's motives. And the more we do this, the deeper the disconnection goes. Brown's observation is worth reflecting on again: "As we take sides, lose trust, and get angrier and angrier, we not only solidify an idea of our enemy, but also start to lose our ability to listen, communicate, and practice even a modicum of empathy."

And the cycle perpetuates itself: The more we distance ourselves from those different from us, the more we distort and distrust them, and the more likely we are to dehumanize them. Once we've dehumanized them, the harder it is to communicate or empathize with them, making us want to distance ourselves even more. And on and on it goes.

Signposts of Brokenness

Disconnection isn't just caused by words that start with the letter D. Beyond distance, distortion, distrust, and dehumanization, we see disconnection rearing its ugly head in so many other ways today—more ways than we can articulate in one chapter. But, in our attempt to propose a constructive lunchroom theology, we want to tease out the causes and manifestations of disconnection so we might better understand the social forces governing the lunchroom. Fear, anger, loneliness, and hate are just a few of the dynamics of disconnection that sociologists describe and that we will examine here.

It's impossible to chart a linear path across these various types of disconnection. Does anger lead to hate? Or is anger an expression of hate? Do we hate people because we're afraid of them? Is loneliness really just a fear of rejection? We're not trying to present a linear equation; we think it's more helpful to view these dynamics as part of an interconnected web with varying points of intersection. Let's explore some of these.

When we were about five months into the COVID-19 pandemic, I (Heather) was talking with one of my pastors, Rachel, about what I felt was an impossible decision I had to make—should I send my first child, a rising kindergartener, to school during a pandemic, when the school system had given little clarity about any safety precautions they would be taking? On the one hand, we could keep my daughter home and oversee "virtual school," which experts were predicting would come with social and intellectual learning loss. On the other hand, we could send her to school, which experts were predicting could turn into endless rounds of quarantine and the risk of spreading the virus to those more medically vulnerable. This choice, which my husband and I had just a few days to make, was months before vaccines were safely available for children.

And I was angry. Angry that the school board wasn't giving us more time to decide. Angry that the county mayor wasn't putting more precautions in place in our area to slow the spread. Angry that my child wasn't going to experience anything resembling "normal" for kindergarten. Angry that my kids had to wear masks. Angry that there was no book on how to parent during a pandemic. Angry that my job was requiring even more from me, making overseeing "virtual school" a near impossibility.

"Rachel," I said to her, "I'm being forced to pick one of these two options, and they're both terrible options. I don't want to have to choose between my daughter's physical health and her intellectual and social health. I want different options to pick from. I'm just so *mad*." And then I burst into tears.

I think what I meant to say was "I'm just so *afraid*."

Afraid I was going to make the wrong choice and mess up my kid irreparably. Afraid that my kid might get infected. Afraid that my kid might infect high-risk family members, friends, or teachers. Afraid that I was overreacting and looking like an idiot. Afraid that we'd all be back in quarantine again. Afraid that my husband or I might get sick and leave our kids without a parent.

I was afraid, but anger was less terrifying than exposing my vulnerability, so I masked my fear with anger. And when I started to come to grips with my fear, I just got angry again that others weren't as afraid as I was, because one of the only things worse than being afraid is being afraid *alone*, being afraid that no one else cares about what you care about. It's the experience the disciples have with Jesus when they wake him up as he sleeps during a storm: "Teacher, do you not care that we are perishing?" (Mark 4:38). Their own fear wasn't the worst thing—it was that Jesus wasn't afraid at all.[25]

Unfortunately, anger and fear thrive in the lunchroom because they're both contagious. Social media and cable news exploit this fact. They prey on our fears, and they know if we get angry, they get clicks. But the more things like anger and fear spread—and they spread *fast*—the more disconnected we become, because despite being contagious and despite our desire to not experience them alone, *they do nothing to connect us*. The same is true of loneliness.

We explained earlier how Brown links the big sort to disconnection. She extends that link to loneliness as well. In fact, data shows that loneliness rates correlate with sorting rates. In 1976, when less than 25 percent of Americans were "sorted" (i.e., lived in landslide counties), only about 20 percent of people reported feeling lonely. In 2016, when 80 percent of Americans were "sorted," more than 40 percent of people reported feeling lonely.[26] We're not saying that one caused the other, but the correlations are significant.

Do you see the troubling paradox? You'd think that we'd feel *more* connected now that we're more closely surrounded with people who are like us. But it doesn't work like that. Surrounding ourselves with others who are like us may bond us over hating the same people or ideas, but it's not genuine belonging. Brown describes the result:

> While we may all be gathered behind the same bunkers of political or social belief and ideology, we're still alone in them. And even worse, we're constantly monitoring ourselves. The looming threat of blowback should we voice an opinion or idea that challenges our bunker mates keeps us anxious. When all that binds us is what we believe rather than who we are, changing our mind or challenging the collective ideology is risky. When a group or community doesn't tolerate dissent and disagreement, it forgoes any experience of inextricable connection. There is no true belonging, only an unspoken treaty to hate the same people. This fuels our spiritual crisis of disconnection.[27]

Fear. Anger. Loneliness. Hate. The combination is reminiscent of Yoda's words to young Anakin, "Fear is the path to the dark side. Fear leads to anger. Anger leads to hate. Hate leads to suffering."[28] Although we might not frame it quite as linearly as our favorite Jedi Master, fear, anger, loneliness, hate, and the like are all forms of disconnection, signposts of brokenness, manifestations of the big sort, and contagions in the lunchroom. And they lead us away from one another rather than toward one another.

The Big Sort . . . and Babel

Social psychologist Jonathan Haidt recently wrote an article, "Why the Past 10 Years of American Life Have Been Uniquely Stupid."[29] We laugh every time we read the title because, well, they *have* been uniquely stupid! Haidt is not a religion scholar, but he aptly uses the story of Babel from Genesis 11 as a metaphor for America in the 2010s. He describes the aftermath of Babel as "people wandering amid the ruins, unable to communicate, condemned to mutual incomprehension." He writes similarly of today: "We are disoriented, unable to speak the same language or recognize the same truth. We are cut off from one another and from the past."

Sociologically, the big sort helps us understand this phenomenon. The law of group polarization helps us understand it. Psychological and social theory on disconnection help us understand it. But we believe there is also a theological explanation for what we're seeing around us. Although our world may indeed be Babel-esque, as Haidt claims, we think the problem even pre-dates Babel.

Moving the Tables:
An Origin Story

*Until you can read the story of Adam and Eve, of
Abraham and Sarah, of David and Bathsheba, as your
own story . . . you have not really understood it.*
FREDERICK BUECHNER

If you don't know what ails you, he can't heal you.
ERIC MINGUS

Disconnection. Fracture. Brokenness. These are all words that describe a
separation. A gap. We believe there's a gap between how the lunchroom operates today and what God originally intended for his creation. But before we can
attend to that gap—or, perhaps more constructively, before we can *narrow* that
gap—we must continue to understand what caused the gap to exist in the first
place. In chapter two we looked at various sociological explanations for societal
fractures. We saw how distance, distortion, and distrust are all manifestations
of disconnection and only serve to exacerbate it; how fear, anger, loneliness,
and the like are powerful forces in the lunchroom that lead us to further division rather than healing. We will continue to assess the fracture in this chapter,
asking, *How did we get this way, and why is our world so destructively divided?* But
now we will approach it through the lens of Scripture. In other words, we'll

explore the theological explanation for why our world resembles a giant high school lunchroom, as well as trace how this theme of fractured relationships plays out repeatedly across the biblical narrative.

If we allow ourselves a deep and honest reflection on Scripture, it reveals a sobering truth. From the days of Noah and Abraham to the exodus and desert wandering, through to the righteous cries of the prophets and the narratives of both Jesus and the early church, we cannot help but see that division has sadly been the way of the world. Even though the groups at the tables have varied across time and place, the world is and always has been a giant, fractured lunchroom.

Always? Well, maybe not always.

In the Beginning . . .

If we go back to the beginning, we see in Genesis 1 and 2 that it hasn't *always* been this way. In the first creation account (Gen. 1:1–2:3), God creates all things by simply speaking them into being. On the sixth day, when God creates humanity, he creates them to reflect his image and gives them a commission to fill and tend the earth (Gen. 1:27–30). This is the culmination of all creation: "God saw everything that he had made, and indeed, it was very good" (Gen. 1:31). In fact, it is so good that God rests from his creative work because it is complete.

In the second creation account (Gen. 2:4–25), we get more details about the fashioning of humanity. In the first chapter of Genesis, the refrain after each day of creation is, "It was good." Here, in the second chapter, we find the first thing that is *not* good. After God makes the man, we get the startling pronouncement, "It is *not good* that the man should be alone" (Gen. 2:18, emphasis added). A solitary, lonely life was not what God intended for humanity. But neither was exact sameness. And so, out of man, God makes not another man, but someone different—woman (Gen. 2:21–22). Woman is like the man, as even the Hebrew words reflect. (The Hebrew word for woman, *ishah*, is the feminine form of the Hebrew word for man, *ish*.) And yet she is distinct. She is not man. They are different.

Different but similar.

Different. Created separately. Given different names. Distinct. (Genesis doesn't emphasize or enumerate the distinctions, and we know better than to try here!)

But similar. Both created in God's image (Gen. 1:27). Both given the same commission to join God in caring for his world (Gen. 1:28–30). Both called to carry it out as partners (Gen. 2:20), not alone. United (Gen. 2:24).[1] And both lacking shame toward one another (Gen. 2:25).

Different but similar. And good. No signs of division or discord. No signs of hierarchy or blame. No anger or injustice or fear or violence.

The table—thus far only set for two—is good. Very good indeed. No fractures in sight.

Until Genesis 3.

A crafty serpent entices the man and woman to disobey God,[2] introducing a new era of humanity characterized by so many things absent in Genesis 1 and 2: shame, division, discord, hierarchy, blame, anger, injustice, fear, violence, and loneliness. Christian theologians from Paul onward have given this phenomenon any number of names—sin, the fall, brokenness, corruption—though none of those terms appear in Genesis 3. Genesis 1 and 2 show God's *good* creative intent for the world, generally, and for human relations, specifically. Genesis 3 and the ever-evolving progression that follows show us the world *not* as God intended it to be.

We see humans experience shame—toward themselves and others (Gen. 3:7, 10). We see fear (Gen. 3:8–10). We see humans refusing to take responsibility for their actions and instead blaming others, including God (Gen. 3:12–13). We see discord between humanity and the earth (Gen. 3:15, 17–19). We see increased physical suffering (Gen. 3:16). We see disordered relationships, characterized by hierarchy. Initially, this focuses on man and woman (Gen. 3:16) but later expands to include all kinds of people.

The chapters that follow in Genesis show this sin and brokenness manifesting in jealousy, fratricide, and increased violence, all of which lead to God's stunning pronouncement of his sorrow in creating humanity: "The LORD was sorry he had made humans on the earth, and it grieved him to his heart" (Gen. 6:6). So God purifies the earth with the flood and starts over with the family of Noah. This new creation echoes the first creation with God's command to "be fruitful and multiply on the earth" (Gen. 8:17; cf. 1:28) and with the repetition that God created humankind "in his own image" (Gen. 9:6; cf. 1:27). But this renewed creation doesn't fare much better than the initial creation, as the narrative quickly devolves into over-indulgence, shame, family division, and—to drastically understate what happened at Babel—misunderstanding (Gen. 9:20–11:9).

Let's pause for a minute and catch our breath. What started as disobedi-ence in Genesis 3 spiraled out of control, wreaking havoc on humanity and God's creation. What was originally a good creation characterized by unity, mutuality, life, and healthy community became a disordered creation characterized by division, discord, death, and dysfunctional community.

The disordered creation feels so familiar to us. Blame, shame, fear, discord, physical suffering, hierarchy, violence, objectification, fear of others—these are the characteristics of the lunchroom from Genesis 3 until today. Though the expressions of these characteristics may vary in different times and places, they are not unique to our world today. This is not a twenty-first-century problem. It's a human problem.

And it is not what God intended.

Two Characters in Every Lunchroom

You may have noticed that we stopped with the story of Babel in Genesis 11. Genesis 11 concludes the first major unit of Genesis, known as the Primeval History, which spans chapters 1 to 11. Genesis 12 begins a new act in the larger story of God, in which God chooses the family of Abraham to bring about blessing to his broken creation. This family takes center stage for the remainder of the book of Genesis.

But this family isn't what you might expect. They are not always obedient. They do bad things (some *very* bad things). Like most fami-lies, they are complex. And they are broken. Really broken. Rabbi Burton Visotzky describes the stories of Abraham's family like this:

> Read simply, Genesis is an ugly little soap opera about a dysfunctional family. Four generations of a family dynasty are charted, their foibles exposed and all the dirty laundry, as it were, hung out in public for millions to see. It is a story about rape, incest, murder, deception, brute force, sex, and blood lust…. Genesis is what spouses hide from the neighbors, hide from the children, hide from each other. The narratives of Genesis are roiling in repressions we refuse to tell our therapists.[3]

So, if you thought God's chosen family was where the brokenness ended, you would be very wrong. Rather, this family is a vivid example of the gap between what is and what should be.

We're going to explore a segment of this chosen family's story through the lens of the lunchroom. Specifically, we want to relate this story to two characters found in every lunchroom—the kid with his back against the wall and the bully pinning him there.

The first character is the kid who's a misfit or an outsider in one way or another. No one is eager to scoot down on the bench to make room for him at their table. Maybe he looks a bit different. Maybe he lives at the trailer park. Maybe he got held back last year. Maybe his clothes are never clean. Maybe he chooses the wall over the tables—the sting of rejection at every lunch table is too much to bear, so he'd rather go at it alone. But all too often, if we dig deeper, the kid with his back against the wall is there because someone has a forearm to his collarbone, forcing the back of his neck to scrape on the rough brick as he gasps for breath, just as his lunch money is stolen for the third time this week.

The kid with his back against the wall exists because another character exists—the bully. The bully is loud and proud—or at least it seems so on the surface. It's more likely that the bully's loudness and apparent proudness are masking a deep insecurity that he hopes no one will ever discover. He makes fun of the kid who doesn't fit at any table because, deep down, he doesn't think he fits anywhere either. He hurts others because he's been hurt, and he hopes that inflicting pain on others will numb his own pain. He has been deeply wounded and dehumanized, so he wounds and dehumanizes others.

Cue Sarai and Hagar.[4]

Like Night and Day

From the outset, these two characters seem as different as night and day or as opposite as John Bender and Claire Standish in the 1985 classic *The Breakfast Club*.[5] (If you haven't experienced it, stop reading now. Go watch it, then resume reading. We'll wait.) Sarai is old, married, rich, and free. Hagar is young, single, poor, and enslaved. They hail from different places—Sarai originally from Ur of the Chaldeans, and Hagar from Egypt. We're not told how Hagar became Sarai's slave, but we find the unlikely pair in Canaan, the land promised for the descendants of Abram *through Sarai*. This is Sarai's turf. She's the cheer captain dating the quarterback of the football team. She holds a position of privilege and power, even in this ancient culture, simply because she is Abram's wife.

Despite all she has going for her, Sarai's prospects remain bleak. The first thing we're told about her, besides her being Abram's wife, is that she is "barren" and has no child (Gen. 11:30). As if recounting it once isn't enough, the narrator emphasizes again, "Sarai, Abram's wife, *bore him no children*" (Gen. 16:1, emphasis added). In a culture where a woman's value is deeply connected to the productivity of her ovaries, Sarai has her back against the wall, as she wears the labels of shame and fear. But instead of remaining there, she decides to put someone else's back against the wall. It's a bold lunchroom move.[6] Naturally, she chooses someone more vulnerable than her; someone easy to exploit; someone without the power to fight back; someone whom she can dehumanize because no one will notice or care; someone whom biblical scholar Wilda Gafney describes as being "on the underside of all the power curves in operation at that time."[7]

She chooses Hagar.

The first descriptor of this woman is that she is an "Egyptian slave" (Gen. 16:1). We're given this descriptor before we're even given her name, and "slave" is the most commonly used label for Hagar throughout the story. Despite being "other" in terms of class, freedom, and ethnicity, she has what Sarai does not—fertility. But, as a slave, she doesn't have control over her own fertility—her mistress does. So, from a position of power, Sarai tells Abram to take her "slave" as a wife (Sarai never uses Hagar's name; she only calls her "slave" or "slave woman") so that Hagar can bear an heir for Sarai. Although this practice was legal in the Ancient Near East at the time,[8] the legality of forced surrogacy hardly softens the blow against Hagar, who ultimately views Sarai with contempt (Gen. 16:4). Sarai uses Hagar as a means to an end, as a ticket out of childlessness; and Hagar, the story tells us, experiences that dehumanization acutely.

Jealousy, exploitation, contempt. The brokenness of the Genesis 3 lunchroom is in full force.

Sarai refuses to take responsibility for what she arranged and instead blames Abram. Abram returns the blame to Sarai—"*Your* slave is in *your* power; do to her as *you* please!" (Gen. 16:6, emphasis added).[9] Sarai responds by afflicting Hagar so badly that she runs away.[10] Biblical scholar Phyllis Trible explains the irony of the Israelite afflicting the Egyptian:

> The verb *afflict* (*'nh*) is a strong one, connoting harsh treatment. It characterizes, for example, the sufferings of the entire Hebrew population in Egypt, the land of their bondage [in Exodus 1:11, 12]. Ironically, here it depicts the torture of a lone Egyptian woman in Canaan, the land of her bondage to the Hebrews. Sarai afflicted Hagar.[11]

Blame, hatred, humiliation. The brokenness of Genesis 3 continues to gain momentum, and Trible's explanation reminds us that the brokenness isn't limited to one people group, one area, or one period of time. As we will continue to show, every group in every time of history manages to perpetuate the lunchroom dynamics, complete with their own tables and bullies and people with their backs against the wall.

The God Who Sees

Hagar has found this version of a bully so completely unbearable that she runs away into the wilderness. An angel finds her by a spring on the way to Shur, a region between Canaan (where she came from) and Egypt (where she's headed). This Egyptian is trying to find her way home, but a divine messenger intercepts her and directs her to return to her mistress (Gen.

16:7–9).[12] With this command, however, the messenger also offers Hagar a promise from the Lord (one that is strikingly similar to the promise to Abraham in Genesis 15:5): Her offspring will be so numerous that they can't be counted (Gen. 16:10). This announcement—to a homeless Egyptian runaway slave—is the first divine announcement of a child and dynasty to a woman in Scripture, making her the "prototype of special mothers in Israel."[13] Sarai never received such an announcement from a divine messenger. Hagar, whose future in servitude looked bleak, is given hope for the survival of her descendants. Her response is the first and only time a person in Scripture names God. Hagar ("the stranger") names God *"El-roi,"* which means "God of seeing" (Gen. 16:13). God sees Hagar when her back is against the wall. (Oh, *to be seen*—there is probably not a more fundamental human longing.)

Upon her return to Sarai and Abram, Hagar gives birth to Ishmael. She then disappears from the narrative for four chapters. Meanwhile, Sarah[14] miraculously conceives and bears her own child (Gen. 21:1–8). Hagar returns in Genesis 21:9, where Ishmael (*her* child through Abraham) and Isaac (*Sarah's* child through Abraham) are now growing up. Both women are now mothers, but Hagar remains poor and enslaved, while Sarah remains rich and free. Despite Sarah's economic advantages, she continues to operate out of a mentality of fear and scarcity, realizing that Hagar's son is a potential threat to her son's inheritance.[15] Frederick Buechner vividly imagines the story Sarah was telling herself: "She was convinced that her upstairs son would have to split his inheritance with Hagar's downstairs brat, so for the second time she nagged Abraham into driving them both out of the house permanently."[16] So Sarah, again the bully, demands that Abraham get rid of Hagar and Ishmael for good. They are sent into the wilderness with nothing more than bread and a skin of water.

Jealously. Distrust. Scarcity. Abuse of power. The brokenness of Genesis 3 rages on.

And yet once more, God sees Hagar when her back is against the wall. When the water is gone, she finds a place for her son to die and then voices her last desperate wish: "Do not let me look on the death of the child"

(Gen. 21:16). But God, who saw her in the wilderness the first time, sees her again and goes beyond what she asks for. Once more, a messenger reassures her that God will make a great nation of her son and directs her to a well of water—she will not see her son's death because he will not die in the wilderness (Gen. 21:17–19). They regain strength and grow, and the story concludes with Hagar finding a wife for Ishmael from among her people in Egypt (Gen. 21:21). Her name never reappears in the Hebrew Scriptures.

Hurt People Hurt People

The point of this story isn't to vilify Sarah or glorify Hagar. Despite their different class, ethnicity, and age, they're both victims of the brokenness that began in Genesis 3. Sarah likely endured decades of ridicule as a barren woman. Heck, her husband tried to pass her off as his sister to the most powerful man in Egypt to save his own skin ... twice (Gen. 12:10–20; 20:1–16)! Sarah hurt Hagar because she'd been hurt. She put someone else's back against the wall because it felt better than having her own there. Sarah's hurt doesn't excuse her behavior, but it does explain it. The story of this Genesis lunchroom is one of a more powerful person redirecting their hurt, shame, and insecurity toward someone to whom a broken culture assigned less power. Rather than breaking the cycle, Sarah perpetuated it.

With our focus on Sarah and Hagar, we failed to hone in on another important character: God. God's character in these chapters is complex, to be sure; and if we're honest, it makes us more than a little uncomfortable in places. But God is not the initiator of this brokenness. He is not the source of the problem. God does not close Sarah's womb, but he does promise to open it. Sarah's lack of trust in this promise leads to further pain. Just as Adam and Eve's disobedience escalated to blame, violence, and death, Sarah's brokenness sends shards flying that hurt those in her vicinity, impacting everyone else in the lunchroom with her brokenness. God does not invite nor cause Sarah to victimize Hagar; Sarah chooses to take out her hurt on Hagar, on someone who is already hurting, rather than to view her as someone with their back against the wall whom she could help.[17]

This pattern of responding to hurt with hurt was never God's intent. In the midst of all the brokenness done to and by these women, God cares for both of them. He sees them both. He opens Sarah's womb, even after her distrust, even after she hurts Hagar. He keeps his promises, despite her doubt. While some may dismiss Hagar as a minor character, her story reveals a vital truth about God's love. Although she is not part of the family God initially chose to bless and is an outsider who could easily be overlooked, God still cares for her, provides for her, and saves her.

Hagar's story is the story of many. As Trible writes:

> As a symbol of the oppressed, Hagar becomes many things to many people. Most especially, all sorts of rejected women find their stories in her. She is the faithful maid exploited, the black woman used by the male and abused by the female of the ruling class, the surrogate mother, the resident alien without legal recourse, the other woman, the runaway youth, the religious fleeing from affliction, the pregnant young woman alone, the expelled wife, the divorced mother with child, the shopping bag lady carrying bread and water, the homeless woman, the indigent relying upon handouts from the power structures, the welfare mother, and the self-effacing female whose own identity shrinks in service to others.[18]

And yet, over the centuries, the church has told Hagar's story so poorly, told it in ways that villainize her and those like her, told it in ways that overlook the real harm done to this woman by God's chosen people, told it in ways that ignore the power dynamics between these two women. Which means we've also told Sarah's story poorly as well. We've failed to acknowledge the depth of her pain and how the power structures don't just hurt the powerless but also the powerful.

Rather than contributing to the healing of a lunchroom full of bullies and kids with their backs against the wall, perhaps the poor ways we have told this and other stories have contributed to this gap between our broken reality and God's good intentions. And perhaps the way we have chosen to tell the stories reveals even bigger failures—failure to recognize that the lunchroom has been in the making since Genesis 3, failure to recognize that overwhelming brokenness has existed *within* God's family from almost the very beginning. This lunchroom dysfunction has been around for a very long time.

The Lunchroom in Jesus' Day

As much as we would like to continue through the Hebrew Scriptures to illustrate time and time again this downward spiral that began in Genesis 3, we need to jump ahead a couple of thousand years. In doing so, we land in the first-century lunchroom—the lunchroom in Jesus' time. The characters have new names, but the dynamics are still those that began in Genesis 3. As the story progressed from Abraham's time to Jesus' time, more tables emerged in the lunchroom, but they were still characterized by defensiveness, jealousy, shame, and the same disregard for those created in God's image. And as it had been before (and still is today!), much of the brokenness is enacted in the name of God.

As we try to understand how we got to where we are today from a theological perspective, let's consider the lunchroom during the time of Jesus. We'll start with the Jewish tables and broaden out from there.

The Jewish Tables

When I (Heather) was in grad school, I remember one professor regularly correcting us if we referred to the period when Jesus lived as "Second Temple Judaism." "Not Judaism, singular," he would insist. "Judaisms, plural." It drove me crazy, but it also accomplished its purpose—it reminded me that the religious world of Jesus wasn't monolithic. It took lots of different tables to hold all the various Jewish beliefs and practices in the first century. My professor wasn't just being a curmudgeonly old scholar nitpicking at his grad students; he was reminding us of the importance of nuance when talking about religious groups. To claim that all Jews during Jesus' time held the same beliefs is about as ludicrous as claiming that all Christians today hold the same beliefs. If someone asked me what Christians today believe about the afterlife or the nature of Scripture, I would probably respond somewhat facetiously, "Which Christians?" The same applies to ancient Judaism, the religious world Jesus and his earliest followers inhabited.[19]

If you strolled through the theological world of Jesus, you would notice the Sadducees in one corner of the ancient lunchroom. They were a priestly group that was sympathetic to Roman power and only accepted the Pentateuch as their Scripture. They were suspicious of the "liberal" Pharisees in the other corner who accepted as Scripture not only the rest of what Christians call the Old Testament (i.e., the historical books, the prophets, and the writings) but even—gasp!—the oral law. If Sadducees were twenty-first-century high schoolers, they'd be huddled around the Fruitopia machine, pointing at the Pharisees and whispering, "How *dare* they go beyond the traditions of Moses!" If the Sadducees' table was in the pro-Roman corner, in the opposite corner was the table with "Sicarii" graffitied onto it. This table was occupied by anti-Roman rebels, a splinter group of Jewish zealots whose violent rebellion against the Roman empire eventually led to the destruction of the temple. If the Sicarii were the fighters, the Essenes were the purists who dragged their lunch table out into the hallway because the whole lunchroom was just too corrupt. Believing the Jewish priesthood was beyond reform and the Roman presence too idolatrous, they established a sectarian, ascetic community in the wilderness, seeking to live out their religious convictions faithfully.

The groups at these lunch tables held different writings as Scripture. They disagreed vehemently about how to relate to the government and surrounding culture. Their theology on key doctrines such as free will, the afterlife, the Messiah, purity, and marriage varied widely. Although the individual groups had certain characteristics in common (e.g., Essenes and Pharisees were both concerned with ritual purity, Zealots and Essenes were both anti-Roman), their differences were substantial enough for them to pull the lunch tables apart and form different groups. And honestly? These were just the tables that were distinct enough to be labeled.[20] These groups were actually pretty small, certainly not constituting a majority of the Jews in Jesus' world. Beyond these groups, the lunchroom reflected a smorgasbord of religious ideologies and practices, with a range of dynamics between the tables—competition, rivalry, ambivalence, disgust, and distrust.

Despite all their disagreements, each of these tables would likely grant that the other tables nonetheless could claim the label "the people of God." Why? Because they held in common the belief in one Creator God who gave Israel the Torah, and their various tables comprised descendants of Abraham and thus constituted the true Israel.

But there was another group who tried to establish that label for their table, who believed they had a rightful claim to the name "God's people," but who were denied that label by most of the Jews described above. That group was the Samaritans. The Samaritans believed *they* were the true descendants of Abraham through the line of Joseph. *They* had the correct version of the Scriptures and the correct interpretation of the Torah. *They* worshiped at the true temple of God at Mount Gerizim. *They* were God's people. The rivalry between the Jewish and Samaritan lunch tables was so strong that they wouldn't associate with one another (John 4:9), they destroyed or defiled the other's holy places, and sometimes even killed one another.[21] Although many today characterize Samaritans as marginalized or oppressed, Jewish New Testament scholar Amy-Jill Levine makes the point that Jesus' Jewish audience more likely would have thought of Samaritans as enemies and oppressors. She says this about the parable of the good Samaritan (Luke 10:25–37): "From the perspective of the man in the ditch, Jewish listeners might balk at the idea of receiving Samaritan aid. They might have thought, 'I'd rather die than acknowledge that one from that group saved me.'"[22] At times, the animosity between these groups resembled that of rival gangs.

Of course, there were also tables in the Jewish section of this first-century lunchroom based on socioeconomic status, how a person made their money, or both. The table most likely to have "traitor" graffitied on it was that of the tax collectors. While nobody today is particularly fond of IRS agents, the hatred of tax collectors by Jews was so intense because they were seen as corrupt traitors exploiting their own people. Theologian and civil rights leader Howard Thurman describes them as despised "because from the inside they had unlocked the door to the enemy"—namely, the Romans. Thurman goes on: "The situation was all the more difficult to bear because the tax collectors tended to be prosperous in contrast with the rest of the people."[23] Not only were they wealthy, but they were wealthy at the expense of their fellow Jews in aid of Rome. Even if they were descendants of Abraham, no one would have been eager to have them at their table.

So Many Other Tables

So far, we've focused on tables in the Jewish section of the first-century lunchroom, but it's important to note that the fractures weren't particularly a *Jewish* phenomenon. If it appears that way, it's only because we've been focusing on the stories from Genesis 12 until the time of Jesus, which, in our Scriptures, are primarily *Jewish* stories. Let us be very clear: This is no indictment of Jews, in particular. This state of the lunchroom is a *human* problem, not a *Jewish* problem.

The lunchroom divisions permeated the larger Greco-Roman world as well. Competing philosophical schools offered varying (and sometimes conflicting) interpretations of the world around them—Platonists, Aristotelians, Epicureans, Cynics, Stoics, and more. Most in the lunchroom were poor, often struggling just to survive, but there would have been a few tables of wealthier elites (called "patrons") who enslaved people or served as benefactors for those with less money and power (called "clients").[24] Masters could treat their slaves however they wanted because they were property. Patrons might provide land to live on, food to eat, or employment for their clients, who were expected to reciprocate with gratitude, loyalty, and praise to improve their patron's social reputation. It was a system that negotiated power, honor, and loyalty without being as dehumanizing as slavery but still operating on a principle of indebtedness.[25] Although some patrons treated their clients well, others were more like the aforementioned bullies who collected scrawny kids' lunch money in return for not shoving them in a locker.

And the list of tables could go on. Greeks often looked down on non-Greeks and viewed them as barbaric. Jews often resented their Gentile Roman oppressors, not only for their overbearing taxation but also for their polytheistic idolatry and emperor worship. Some Jews in and around the land of Israel viewed Jews in the diaspora (those scattered among Gentile nations who were more likely to adopt the Greek language and participate in Greek civic life) as failing to obey the covenant and follow the wisdom of the Torah. The Jews in Israel were skeptical of diaspora Jews' ability to maintain their distinctive Jewish identity (e.g., monotheism, Sabbath observance, dietary laws) among Gentiles.[26] The depth and breadth of the fractures in the first-century lunchroom are enough to make our heads spin.

And Yet . . .

Despite all this, we must remember that *it hasn't always been this way*. God's original creation didn't have divided tables or disconnection or dehumanization. It wasn't broken. But from Genesis 3 onward, both within God's people and beyond, the brokenness became more severe. The gap kept widening. The lunchroom continued to fracture. More and more tables were set up, each making sure they weren't too close to the one next to them. The distance between the tables led to distorted views of the other tables. The distortions naturally led to distrust, which easily spiraled into dehumanization. Bullies gained power and used and abused those who didn't fit in at any of the tables. There were plenty of kids with their backs against the wall.

And yet God was not content to leave the lunchroom as it was. In fact, he was so committed to repairing the lunchroom that he came there himself to show us a better way. The very act of Jesus entering the lunchroom gives us hope that the gap between God's original intention and the ongoing brokenness of our world can begin to close.

To Roy's Question . . .

We all do what we know to do until we learn to do something different.
ODESSA SETTLES

How can this be?
NICODEMUS

In August 2020, as the world was in the throes of a devasting pandemic and we all endured our own personal lockdown purgatories, a little television show premiered. A "fish out of water" tale,[1] *Ted Lasso* tells the story of an American college football coach who is surprisingly hired to train an English Premier League football (soccer) team, despite having no previous experience or knowledge of the sport. Lasso is recruited by the club's owner, Rebecca, in the hope that he will fail miserably and, in doing so, enact revenge upon her unfaithful ex-husband, the previous owner of the team. However, her plan fails, as, against all odds, Ted coaches the players to victory and slowly changes the team culture through his folksy, homespun wisdom and humor.

Ted Lasso became somewhat of a phenomenon, becoming the most-watched series ever on Apple TV+[2] and garnering several awards over the next few years. The show's reviews stood out from the normal critiques of a run-of-the-mill episodic comedy:

Above all odds, *Ted Lasso* chipped away at my skepticism until there was none left—just like the character himself does to everyone he meets. At a time when just about everything feels catastrophic, there's something undeniably satisfying about spending some time with good people who are just trying to be the best they can, on and off the field.[3]

Ted Lasso is the wholesome American hero we need ... the landscape of television has felt kind of gloomy, so imagine my surprise when I turned on the TV to *Ted Lasso* and felt a swelling of a now unfamiliar emotion—hope.[4]

Every step of the way, *Ted Lasso* proves to be comforting and entertaining and somehow both a distraction and a reminder that kindness is out there, not just on this fictional show, not just across the pond, but deep in the heart of America too.[5]

We don't disagree with any of these assessments, but what if there's something about the show that is even more compelling than people trying to be the best they can or reminding us that kindness is out there? What was it about this show that, even during the despair of a global pandemic and the vitriol rising from worldwide politics, somehow brought so many a sense of respite? Ultimately, whether intentionally or unintentionally, we believe that *Ted Lasso* came to represent *hope in the ability to change*. That's the story *Ted Lasso* is really telling. In dealing with issues and topics rarely dealt with by episodic comedies, this show provides a narrative for every main character to experience personal growth and healing, perhaps none as overtly as Roy Kent.

Roy Kent is a player in the twilight of his career, known for his physical play on the field and his intense gruffness and crudeness in the locker room. (One in every five or six words spoken by Roy is the "F" word.) Throughout the show's three seasons, either while playing on the team or in his role as an assistant coach, no one seems to have more of an evolutionary arc than Roy. In the final episode of the series, he asks a crucial question, one we believe is the essential question the previous thirty-four episodes were asking: "Can people change?"

Here's the scene:

Roy: For the past year, I've busted my f—ing ass trying to change. But apparently, I haven't done f—ing sh—t, 'cause ... I'm still me.

Ted: Wait. Did you wanna be someone else?

Roy: Yeah. Someone better. (Long pause.) Can people change?[6]

After a lengthy exchange between multiple characters on the possibility of people really changing and the belief that change is not about being perfect, the conclusive answer comes from the team's director of operations, Leslie Higgins:

Human beings are never gonna be perfect, Roy.
The best we can do is to keep asking for help and accepting it when you can.
And if you keep on doing that, you'll always be moving towards better.[7]

This book is founded upon the belief that change is possible, that the state of the lunchroom doesn't have to remain as it is today, and that we can begin to close the gap between the way things are and the way God intended them to be. Another way *is* possible.

Now that we have explored the sociological and theological reasons for the lunchroom reality of our world, we want to begin asking what a better lunchroom could look like. How can we shift our broken lunchroom paradigms and set about seeing the world anew? Is there a way of living in the world that moves beyond the big sort? A way of relating to one another that's different from the default of the Three Ds of Disconnection—distance, distortion, and distrust? A way of breaking the destructive repetitive cycle we read throughout the story of Scripture and that is so evident in the world around us?

In this chapter and the next, we are asking you to radically rethink how, as followers of Jesus, we can begin to live something inherently distinct from the prevailing lunchroom culture of our world. We believe Jesus' teachings and his way of gathering people are fundamental in helping us see what a new kind of lunchroom could look like. And so, to attempt to enter this radical rethinking Jesus calls us toward, we would like to ask you a question ...

If You Could Pick One Day

If you had the extraordinary ability to transport yourself anywhere in time and space, where would you go? More specific to the topic at hand, if you could transport yourself into the middle of any of the stories of Jesus, which place, time, or moment would you choose? If you could suspend the laws of nature and travel to one specific day in the life of Jesus, where would you land? His birth? Death? Resurrection? Maybe his ascension? Perhaps you'd want to drop in on a particular miracle or healing or an encounter with Jesus' friends or even enemies? If you could magically find your way to that place at that time in the narrative of Jesus, which moment would you pick?

I (Mark) have actually spent way too much time considering my answer to this question. My conclusion is that I would pick the Thursday evening, the day before the crucifixion, just before the sun goes down, right before Jesus is arrested and led to the most horrific of deaths.[8] And I would want the ability to hear, see, and feel everything anyone else was hearing, seeing, or feeling. There are just *so many* things happening on that Thursday night of the week that we call "Holy," and I would love to find myself in the middle of it all.

All four Gospels give an account of this day, but John gives us a slow-motion portrayal of those last few hours—almost a third of the book of John is devoted to this one night. He provides long stretches of dialogue and notes the emotions of some of those involved, drawing the reader into the narrative. John 13–17 gives an intimate account of what will turn into Jesus' most anguished night on earth.

In those last moments with his closest friends, Jesus washes their feet, predicts his betrayal, and freaks them all out by telling them he will be leaving soon. Addressing the disciples' fear of the unknown, Jesus says things like: "Do not let your hearts be troubled" (John 14:1); "I will ask the Father, and he will give you another Advocate, to be with you forever" (John 14:16); and again, "Do not let your hearts be troubled, and do not let them be afraid" (John 14:27). We come to learn these words are quite appropriate, as there will be *plenty* for them to fear in the next few hours: They will be confronted by a group of armed soldiers, see Jesus brutally tortured, and witness the death of their teacher and friend. Those closest to Jesus are about to have their world torn apart right before their eyes. Everything they have known for the last three years is going to change. Jesus will be leaving, and *nothing* will ever be the same.

A Conversation from the Center of the Universe

The four Gospels tell us that Jesus prayed *a lot*. For most of those prayers, though, Jesus was alone, which means we don't know what he was actually praying. But in John 17—as Jesus prepares his followers for his impending death—his friends get to listen in, and, as a result, so do we. We get to listen in on a conversation at the center of the universe: God the Son opens his heart to God the Father. Speculating on the emotional state of Jesus in John 17, missiologist Lesslie Newbigin says,

> When a man is going on a long journey he will find time on the eve of his departure for a quiet talk with his family, and—if he is a man of God—will end by commending to God not only himself and his journey, but also the family whom he leaves behind. Very surely will this be so if his journey is the last journey.[9]

At the end of this Thursday evening, Jesus speaks his final words to his closest friends before this, *his last journey*. On this night, Jesus knows death is imminent; and just minutes before his arrest, at the end of the most intimate of evenings, Jesus prays. John 17 is this prayer, and this prayer is where Jesus most clearly articulates his desire for a reordered lunchroom.

Weirdly, this beautiful and compassionate prayer can at times read like the instructions a parent might give to a babysitter. Jesus prays that the kids get along while he's gone: "Holy Father, protect them in your name that you have given me, so that they may be one, as we are one" (v. 11). He also prays that the kids be kept safe: "I am not asking you to take them out of the world, but I ask you to protect them from the evil one" (v. 15). Even more strange, he not only gives directives in his prayer for those who have been with him over the last few years but also for his *future kids*: "I ask not only on behalf of these but also on behalf of those who believe in me through their word, that they may all be one. As you, Father, are in me and I am in you, may they also be in us, so that the world may believe that you have sent me" (vv. 20–21). Jesus prayed for his future followers, which is to say that *Jesus prayed for us.*

"One" from Two Angles

Among the many and powerful things Jesus is doing in this prayer, he is giving two different angles on "oneness." The first is Jesus' desire for us to have a oneness with the Father as he has: "So that they may be one, as we are one" (v. 11). The oneness he desires for us reaches deep into the being of God and finds its source in the relationship between Father and Son. Jesus is asking for the restoration of oneness between humanity and God that was present in Genesis 1–2 but that was broken and distorted in Genesis 3. The second angle on the word "one" in this John 17 prayer, and the obvious reason for us to focus so much attention on this prayer is Jesus' emphasis on the "oneness" among his followers—a oneness that not only unites all those who come to believe with one another but also unites them with Jesus' first followers. As Newbigin explains,

> The prayer of Jesus is for a unity which … will enable the world to know the love of God not just as an idea or a doctrine but as a palpable reality experienced in the supernatural love which holds believers together in spite of all their human diversities.[10]

Notable in Jesus' prayer is his emphasis on how the disciples' oneness impacts the entire world. "The world" is mentioned eighteen times in this prayer, showing Jesus' deeper concern with the mission of God in the world.[11] This isn't surprising, considering how much "the world" was a part of Jesus' mission throughout John. New Testament scholar Lindsey Trozzo elaborates:

> Jesus was sent to enlighten *the world*, to take away the sin of *the world* (1:29), to give life to *the world* (3:16–17; 6:33, 51), to save *the world* (4:42; 12:47), to show *the world* the love he shares with the Father (14:31; 17:23). Jesus asks in his last prayer, "I in them and you in me, that

they may become completely one, so that *the world* may know that you
have sent me and have loved them even as you have loved me" (17:23).
Through the disciples, the world has the chance to receive the one who
sent them (Jesus), and thus the one who sent him (God). Unity with
Jesus not only enlists the disciples in the mission but also enables them
to complete it."[12]

Thus, Jesus' parting prayer is not only a plea to the Father but also a prepara-
tion for the disciples on how to live once he departs. That is, his prayer is as
much *commission* as *petition*: "As you have sent me into the world, so I have
sent them into the world" (v. 18). New Testament scholar Marianne Meye
Thompson explains how their oneness has a larger purpose:

> The disciples are not only to look inward or to each other. Empowered
> by the Spirit, and in their communion with the Father and the Son, they
> are to look outward to the world that God loves. They are sent into the
> world even as Jesus was sent, bearing witness to the light and life of God
> (17:18).[13]

As they are sent into a watching world, Jesus hopes they will display both
kinds of oneness, knowing that the second is impossible without the first.

In this final prayer before his arrest, Jesus establishes how high the
stakes really are when it comes to the oneness he's talking about. The
world's belief depends on his followers' (and future followers') oneness
(vv. 20–21). To put it another way, if the world is going to see God's good
intent for all creation, God's intent for wholeness over brokenness, and
his intent for connection over disconnection, they will see it through his
followers' *oneness.*

In other words, we have to work on our own attitudes in the lunchroom, our own tables, our own bullies and kids with their backs against the
wall. Living in the lunchroom in oneness with God and fellow believers is
the *starting* point of God's all-inclusive mission because it offers everyone
else a more compelling vision for how we can live.[14] Transformation *begins*
with us, but it doesn't end with us.

But Did He Really Mean It?

In light of this prayer (and in light of the big idea of this book), we should probably consider a few simple questions: Did Jesus *really* mean and believe what he prayed? Is John 17 *really* as formative a vision as we need it to be? Did he *really* expect that, with our differences, we would find a way to push the tables together in our fractured lunchroom world?

Without a doubt, we say yes to all these questions. Jesus meant what he said, and that premise forms the foundation of the rest of this book. This is the vision that has been set out before us. It's the proverbial carrot dangled a few feet in front. And in the current state of this broken lunchroom, it seems this carrot is moving ever further from our grasp.

This reality forces us back to Roy's question: "Can people actually change?" Can we, as followers of Jesus, actually embody the prayer that Jesus prayed? It's one thing for Jesus to pray this for us, it's another for us to say we believe Jesus actually meant what he prayed, and it's still another for us to actually accomplish what Jesus prayed for. Is there any chance, if we took this prayer seriously, that we could close the existing gap between who we are and who we were intended to be? Can we find new hope, a new aspiration, in the prayer of Jesus in John 17, and can that hope lead to deep and consummate change? That is the real question.

It goes without saying that if we want that deep and consummate change, we cannot keep doing what we've been doing. We must be open to a different way of seeing the lunchroom, ourselves, and others and aspire to something new. It's not enough just to *understand* the sociological and theological origins of the lunchroom. Being able to name the big sort or agreeing that the brokenness of Genesis 3 isn't God's intent for our world is no guarantee that anything will change. Even agreeing that Jesus actually meant what he said in John 17 will not suffice. Theoretical knowledge or agreement isn't enough to create change.

No, deep, consummate change happens when we decide that the vision set out before us is something we so desire, so aspire to, that we are willing to make space in our life for it to actually happen. The belief that another way is possible is good; the aspiration to make that happen is even better.

But both must be accompanied by a commitment to *do* what is required to bring that vision to fruition, or nothing will change. If we are not willing to rethink our complicity and restructure our role in this tragically broken lunchroom, and if we are not willing to reassess our misplaced values and pursue a better version of ourselves, Jesus' prayer will never be fulfilled.

We believe that Jesus really did mean what he said and that another, better way is possible. We also believe that world-altering change can happen when those words of Jesus are taken just as seriously as he meant them to be taken. We are thoroughly convinced that we need to be "always moving towards the better," as Higgins said. And to answer Roy's question, if we may, "Yes, Roy, people can change. People can really f——ing change."

And Now, to Nicodemus's Question

In John 3, the religious leader Nicodemus pays Jesus a visit in the shadows of night (John 3:1–21). By this point, Jesus had gained some notoriety for his water-to-wine miracle and his whip-wielding temple incident, and Nicodemus—recognizing Jesus as a fellow religious teacher—asks him some searching questions. It seems that Nicodemus believes there might be something more to his faith than he has experienced thus far, that a different way might be possible.[15]

When Nicodemus rightly acknowledges that the signs Jesus had performed signify that he comes from God, Jesus responds, "Very truly I tell you, no one can see the kingdom of God unless they are born again" (John 3:3 NIV). We imagine a long, somewhat awkward pause as Nicodemus ponders Jesus' words. Although being "born again" is a relatively common phrase in many Christian circles today, it wasn't a familiar concept in ancient Judaism and thus wouldn't make sense to Nicodemus (or any other first-century Jew for that matter). Nicodemus has to decide how to respond to something he's not sure he even understands.

And so he takes the humble approach and asks for clarification: "How can anyone be born after having grown old? Can one enter a second time into the mother's womb and be born?" (John 3:4). What the NIV translates as "born again" (v. 3), the NRSVUE translates as "born from above." Both are viable translations of the Greek adverb *anōthen*, and in fact the double meaning is part of Nicodemus's misunderstanding. Nicodemus was taking the birthing metaphor in a temporal sense (being born a second time), whereas Jesus meant it to refer to the source of the birth (from above—that is, from God). Jesus is giving some insight into the deep and consummate change it will take to embody the unity he calls us to in John 17—the deep unity humans can experience with God by being born from above. And so, although *Ted Lasso's* Leslie Higgins may be right—we can "always be moving towards better"—it is only oneness with God that enables transformational metamorphosis, a caterpillar-to-butterfly change.[16] Our oneness with God brings a much deeper change than the self-help books promise. It is a unity *with* God and *from* God that, in turn, has the potential to produce oneness with one another, a oneness so deep that the world will know that God sent Jesus and that God loves them even as much as he loves the Son (John 17:23). Sit with that for a minute.

Jesus tells Nicodemus that the kingdom of God is so radical that it can only be entered by undergoing something equally revolutionary: *a new birth, being born a second time, being born from above.* Jesus elaborates further on this new birth: "Very truly, I tell you, no one can enter the kingdom of God without being born of water and Spirit" (John 3:5). Here he is pointing to God's Spirit, which will equip and empower them to live in unity after Jesus returns to the Father and thus allow them to accomplish the mission he gives them.

Jesus' encounter with Nicodemus was not a theological debate on the details of the Law or the Prophets; instead, Jesus was calling this curious religious leader *to a deep and consummate change.* A change from the inside out. A change that makes room for another way of seeing God and the world. A change that is rooted in the ways of Jesus, both in what Jesus said about tables and in whom he shared tables with. A change that ultimately has the potential to make Jesus' vision for the lunchroom a reality.

There's Still Room

The kingdom of God ought to reshape our vision
of what matters and who matters.
RUSSELL MOORE

This is what God's kingdom is like: a bunch of outcasts
and oddballs gathered at a table, not because they are rich
or worthy or good, but because they are hungry, because
they said "yes." And there's always room for more.
RACHEL HELD EVANS

In John 17, Jesus lays out a vision for how his followers were to relate to one another as part of the lunchroom. It's a vision rooted in oneness with God and oneness with those who believe and follow Jesus. It's a vision that, if enacted well, has the potential to change the wider lunchroom world.

The work of the church is not to try to manage and control all the other tables in the lunchroom. Nor should Christians express our oneness by huddling up all together to avoid being "corrupted" by the other (non-churchy) tables. Neither dominance nor isolation are a part of Jesus' vision for how to operate in the lunchroom. Oneness with God and oneness with other followers of Jesus means that *the transformation must begin at our own tables.* (If memory serves, someone important once said something about worrying about the plank in our own eye before going after the speck in someone else's.)

Before Jesus prayed for his followers' oneness in John 17, he spent a great deal of time modeling how to counterculturally shape the wider lunchroom, how to share tables with both those who were trying to follow God and those who weren't. Jesus shows us a whole new way of viewing the lunchroom—what its seating chart could look like, how we underestimate the capacity of the tables, and who we might need to consider sharing tables with. In this chapter we want to explore the depth and breadth of Jesus' vision for the lunchroom by looking at *who* he ate with and *what* he said about the table. These stories provide more details of his vision both for those who believe and those who don't—for those at our tables and those at other tables. They may even cause us to question whether those are helpful distinctions!

Jesus' Lunch Buddies

One of the striking things about Jesus in the Gospels, especially in the Gospel of Luke, is that he eats … a lot. As lovers of good food, we're sad to report that the Gospel writers rarely tell us *what* Jesus ate. Besides a few references to bread and fish, we're left to our own imaginations. Would Jesus' Instagram feed be full of figs and honey? Or was he more of a lentil stew kind of guy? Religion scholars Matthew Croasmun and Miroslav Volf, in a book entirely about food and meals in Luke, reflect on what Jesus does and doesn't comment on at meals:

> Jesus hardly says a word about the food or the wine. There's not a single comment that could count as a culinary insight. His comments are about foot-washing, greeting kisses at the door, seating charts, invitation lists, and who gets invited back. *He is consistently concerned with who is at the table and how they are relating to one another.*[1]

It is safe to say that Jesus had a keen sense of *commensality*, a term that means "eating at the same table."[2] Archaeologist Susanne Kerner and anthropologist Cynthia Chou explain further: "In its broader general meaning, [commensality] describes eating and drinking together in a common physical or social setting. Eating is, in all cultures, a social activity and commensality is undeniably one of the most important articulations of human sociality…. Commensality is about creating and reinforcing social relations."[3]

With Jesus, the table was always about so much more than the food. New Testament scholar Eric Barreto puts it another way, explaining that "the meals Luke narrates are symbols and embodiments of belonging."[4] Thus, as Barreto explains, rather than providing us with specific lists of how to do meals, Luke instead tells stories that "narrate *imaginative possibilities of belonging*."[5] When we look closely, we see that "our imaginations are too narrow and that, in light of God's welcome, still much more is possible than we can even imagine. The stories connote what it feels like to embrace and be embraced at a bountiful table."[6] So, when Jesus ate, who was he with? What boundaries of inclusion or exclusion did Jesus explore at the table? To whom did he offer belonging? We'll answer those questions primarily by looking at the Gospel of Luke because, as New Testament scholar Robert Karris puts it, "In Luke's Gospel Jesus is either going to a meal, at a meal, or coming from a meal"[7] (which, if you ask us, sounds a lot like the life of a typical high schooler).

Tax Collectors and Sinners

Much of the criticism Jesus received was due to him eating with tax collectors and sinners. We talked about tax collectors briefly in chapter three, but we want to explore more deeply who these tax collectors were, why the Gospel writers often associate them with sinners, and, most importantly, the significance of Jesus choosing to eat with them.

Tax collectors were among the most detested folks in Judaism because they didn't just work for the oppressors, the Romans; they exploited their own people, the Jews, for the Romans and thus contributed to the oppression of their own people.[8] Often, the tax collectors would do this by deliberately overtaxing so they could take a cut of the profit for themselves, a practice to which the New Testament testifies. Zacchaeus was a chief tax collector who, when called to aspire to more by Jesus, offered to pay back fourfold whatever he had defrauded people (Luke 19:1–10). This would be a strange offer had he not actually defrauded people. Pastor and activist Dominique DuBois Gilliard paints a picture of chief tax collectors as ruthless and greedy:

> [They] extracted profit from the common tax collectors they supervised, who existed on a lower rung of the systemic food chain of oppression. Comparable to white-collar criminals today, chief tax collectors' fiscal flourishing was rooted in systemic sin. They profited from a depraved system that ensured the rich would get richer by oppressing the public and extorting the poor.[9]

Paying taxes was bad enough. But to pay more than you owed when you barely had enough, just to help a traitor line his pockets as he channeled your money to Rome was just plain awful.[10] And yet Jesus shared tables with tax collectors.

After inviting himself to Zacchaeus's home, those around Jesus complained that he had "gone to be the guest of … a sinner" (Luke 19:7). Gilliard argues that the infamous Sunday School song has led to a common misconception that Zacchaeus's height was the primary impediment keeping him from Jesus. (He "was a wee little man, and a wee little man was he," after all.) Gilliard contends, however, that "Zacchaeus was also unable to see Jesus because his peers were repulsed by him and saw him as their enemy. They therefore refused to assist, touch, or make room for him. Zacchaeus, because of his economic exploitation, found himself physically and socially isolated from both Jesus and his community."[11] But Jesus wanted a seat at Zacchaeus's table, even when no one else did.

Multiple times in the Gospels, folks get upset about Jesus sharing tables with such unsavory people. We see this among the crowd in the Zacchaeus story. We see it when the Pharisees and scribes grumble in Luke 15:2, saying, "This fellow welcomes sinners and eats with them." It's important to be clear here that the Pharisees weren't using the term "sinner" in the universal way many Christians use it today, when we say something like, "Well, we're all sinners!" No, "sinner" was a category for *others*. Barreto explains it like this:

["Sinners"] doesn't signify all of us or even most of us. It points to "those people," people with whom we would not want to associate. "Sinners" dwell on the edge of their communities; they are people without a place, people with whom most of us would not want to share a table. Sinners do not belong. It matters very little what they may have done in their past. It matters very little what their behavior is. It's their identity that matters. When we see "sinners," we do not see neighbors, friends, siblings, or fellow guests at a table; we see a body to exclude.[12]

And yet Jesus ate with sinners. He saw them as more than bodies to exclude. And doing so earned him a reputation. Jesus summarizes the lunchroom gossip about himself in Luke 7:34: "You say, 'Look, a glutton and a drunkard, a friend of tax collectors and sinners!'"

Jesus had a different vision of the lunchroom and commensality—one that ultimately extended an invitation for true belonging, regardless of the set of criteria defined by society. New Testament scholar Joachim Jeremias explains it like this:

Jesus' meals with the publicans [tax collectors] and sinners, too, are not only events on a social level, not only an expression of his unusual humanity and social generosity and his sympathy with those who were despised, but had an even deeper significance. They are an expression of the mission and message of Jesus (Mark 2.17) .... The inclusion of sinners in the community of salvation, achieved in table fellowship, is the most meaningful expression of the message of the redeeming love of God.[13]

Even though it earned him an unsavory reputation, even though it upset some of the good religious influencers of the day, even though it likely embarrassed his family, even though it most definitely involved some awkward conversations, even though it made it harder for him to be accepted at other tables, Jesus' vision for a more expansive lunchroom table meant that the sinners and tax collectors had a seat at the table. The offer of belonging was extended to *all*. Ultimately it was Jesus' presence at Zacchaeus's table that transformed both Zacchaeus and his community. Wrongs were righted, and the one everyone loved to hate was radically changed. Perhaps we shouldn't be surprised that fractures at and between tables can be healed by the very act of sharing tables.

Pharisees

Although some in Jesus' day were bothered by him pulling up a chair at the "sinners" table, they probably didn't think twice about him eating with Pharisees. In a minute we'll eavesdrop on one of Jesus' dinner-table conversations at a Pharisee's house, but first we need to understand this religious group from Jesus' day, as they are easily one of the most misunderstood characters in all of Scripture.[14]

As we described in chapter three, Pharisees were one of several important sects in Judaism during the time of Jesus, along with others like the Sadducees, Essenes, and Herodians. Most sects were relatively small, though Josephus, a Jewish historian from the first century, emphasized the Pharisees' popularity among the Jewish people.[15] Christian stereotypes of Pharisees as "xenophobic, self-righteous, elitist, legalistic, money-loving, judgmental, unseeing hypocrites"[16] (or as some combination of those characteristics) might make the Pharisees' popularity surprising to modern readers. Did *some* Pharisees embody *some* of those characteristics? Sure. Luke calls the Pharisees who ridiculed Jesus "lovers of money" (Luke 16:14), and Jesus says they are "full of greed and wickedness" (Luke 11:39). But before we generalize from a few individuals to the entire group, we should ask whether any followers of Jesus today are xenophobic, self-righteous, elitist, legalistic, money-loving, judgmental, unseeing hypocrites. Do such individuals make us attribute those characteristics to *all* Christians? We hope not. We need to apply the same nuance and charity when analyzing the Pharisees.

Though the Pharisees led the people on religious matters, particularly on how to interpret God's word in their current circumstances, they were not formal clergy, as many might assume. Rather, as New Testament scholar Amy-Jill Levine describes them, they were "lay leaders who set themselves a high standard."[17] They were known for their righteousness, ritual purity, and commitment to God's law. Jesus himself recognizes their high standards when he instructs his followers that their righteousness should exceed that of the scribes and Pharisees (Matt. 5:20). These lay leaders were known for emphasizing faithfulness to God's Word and encouraging God's people to keep their covenant with God—things I think we can all agree are good, even if the Pharisees took it too far sometimes. These pastoral concerns about what it meant to honor their covenant with God and what it meant to live as a faithful Jew when their culture was trying to erase their identity were at the heart of why they cared about what people ate, when people worked, and who people shared tables with. (On that note, have we ever considered whether the culture wars today are driven, at least in part, by a genuine pastoral concern by God's people to live out their faith and protect their identity?)

Luke's portrait of the Pharisees is multifaceted.[18] Some of the more positive interactions include them inviting Jesus to dinner (Luke 7:36–50, 11:37–54, 14:1–24) and warning Jesus about Herod's desire to kill him (Luke 13:31). We also know from Luke's second volume, Acts, that some Pharisees are a part of the Christian community (Acts 15:5). Furthermore, the Pharisees had important points of agreement with Jesus on topics like resurrection and their hopes for the coming kingdom of God.[19] In fact, New Testament scholar Mark Allan Powell proposes that Jesus "probably had more in common with the Pharisees than with any other Jewish group of his day, which could explain why most of his arguments were with them: they had enough in common to make debate possible."[20]

However, not all the Pharisees' interactions with Jesus were so favorable. Jesus concluded one dinner with a series of woes against the host (Luke 11:42–44), which included Jesus telling him that the Pharisees "neglect[ed] justice and the love of God" (v. 42). Jesus criticized another Pharisee for failing to be a good host (Luke 7:45–46). Elsewhere, the Pharisees accused Jesus of blasphemy (Luke 5:17–21), complained about Jesus eating with sinners (Luke 5:30; 15:2), and questioned Jesus' interpretation of Jewish traditions (Luke 6:1–11). Jesus' relationship with the Pharisees was complex, and their times together around the table were sometimes marked with tension.

A key conflict between Jesus and the Pharisees related to who they should share tables with. Jesus ate with the Pharisees, and they ate with him, but the Pharisees took issue with Jesus sharing meals with sinners. Scholars debate *why* they took issue with this, but we find Powell's reasoning most compelling: "The best explanation for the controversy over Jesus' association with the wicked is that he was regarded by his contemporaries as communicating a divine acceptance of sinners who did not appear to have repented."[21] Although some sinners *did* repent because they shared a table with Jesus (as we saw earlier with Zacchaeus), it's not clear that all of them did. Had they always repented, we assume the Pharisees would have been delighted, as they certainly wanted such transformation. The difference is that the Pharisees seemed to view repentance as a *prerequisite* for sharing tables with sinners.

But Jesus didn't share the same view. His vision for the lunchroom refused the labels. It refused to accept the notion that sharing a table with someone was the same as approving of every aspect of their life or theology. It refused to treat sharing tables as transactional, where table fellows were viewed merely as targets for conversion. No, as we'll see shortly, Jesus rejected a vision of the lunchroom that expected reciprocity or that came with strings attached. Jesus' lunch buddies included both religious and non-religious—those considered saints and those considered sinners—those loved by the community and those despised by it. And although those groups wouldn't ordinarily share tables with one another, Jesus was committed to sharing tables with them both.

What Jesus Teaches about the Table

In Jesus' time, many aspects of people's lives were structured around social stratification—rich/poor, male/female, master/slave. Similar social and economic categories are present in our world today, and they function similarly—separating who's in from who's out.[22] In Jesus' day, meals both revealed and reinforced the social structure. Part of this derived from who you ate with and what you ate, but part of it also related to the concept of reciprocity, which kept everyone bound to one another. Dinner invitations, for instance, came with unwritten expectations. If you accepted an invitation to dinner, you were expected to extend a comparable one (or something else comparable). I'll scratch your back if you scratch mine. Since the poor couldn't exactly repay the rich with a nice dinner, *if* they were invited and *if* they accepted (two big "ifs"), they would *still* be expected to reciprocate, even if in a different way—with praise of the host's generosity, for instance.[23] It was a complex web of social dynamics, with honor and reciprocity governing those dynamics.

In Luke 14, Jesus attends a dinner party hosted by a prominent Pharisee. After telling a parable in response to everyone choosing their places of honor at the table (vv. 8–11), Jesus turns to the host and says:

> "When you give a luncheon or a dinner, do not invite your friends or
> your brothers and sisters or your relatives or rich neighbors, in case they
> may invite you in return, and you would be repaid. But when you give a
> banquet, invite the poor, the crippled, the lame, and the blind. And you
> will be blessed because they cannot repay you, for you will be repaid at
> the resurrection of the righteous."
>
> LUKE 14:12–14

We assume you've heard the advice, "Don't bite the hand that feeds you." Jesus just toasted that hand, put some jam on it, and ate it for dinner. His advice here is a scathing critique of the host, who had invited his friends, family, and rich neighbors for dinner.

When Jesus says not to invite your friends, relatives, and rich neighbors, he's describing a person's inner circle. These are relationships of equality, mutuality, and easy reciprocity. These are all folks who can return the favor, invite you back, repay you for your generosity, and make it look like you're with the "right" crowd. These are the people we hunker down with in the big sort—those with shared values, religious beliefs, and expectations for life. But that's not what our tables are supposed to look like, Jesus says. Instead, he tells the host to invite the poor, crippled, lame, and blind. Anyone who was paying attention earlier in Luke would remember that in Jesus' very first sermon, he said that the Spirit of the Lord was upon him to bring good news to those same groups—the poor, the captives, the blind, and the oppressed (Luke 4:18–19). And anyone who was paying attention earlier in the Bible would know that Jesus' sermon was a quotation from Isaiah 61:1–2. These people being invited to the table isn't a new thing. It is at the very heart of who God is and who he always has been.

Our tables are to look like Jesus' table. The reason we invite the poor, the crippled, the lame, and the blind (and the Pharisees, tax collectors, and sinners!) is "because they cannot repay [us]" (Luke 14:14). Jesus is rejecting the "strings attached" reciprocity model of his day.[24] And while Jesus does promise that "you will be repayed at the resurrection of the righteous," the reason the guest list looks like this has to do with the nature of God. God, of course, is the ultimate host.[25] If God's generosity and inclusion were predicated on our ability to repay him, the model would fall apart because no one could ever repay God. And so, just as Jesus instructed in Luke 6 to "be merciful, just as your Father is merciful" (v. 36), generosity and inclusion are to flow out of us as we appreciate God's expansive mercy. It all goes back to God's character.

At Jesus' mention of the resurrection of the righteous (Luke 14:14)—a reference to the time when God will make all things right, when his kingdom will be fully here—one of the dinner guests proclaims, "Blessed is anyone who will eat bread in the kingdom of God!" (v. 15). This guy's enthusiasm seems to be rooted in the assumption that he will—obviously—be invited to eat bread in the kingdom of God. He's certain of his place at the table, of his place on the guest list.

But Jesus can't just leave it at that. He tells this parable:

> "Someone gave a great dinner and invited many. At the time for the dinner he sent his slave to say to those who had been invited, 'Come, for everything is ready now.' But they all alike began to make excuses. The first said to him, 'I have bought a piece of land, and I must go out and see it; please accept my regrets.' Another said, 'I have bought five yoke of oxen, and I am going to try them out; please accept my regrets.' Another said, 'I have just been married, and therefore I cannot come.' So the slave returned and reported this to his master. Then the owner of the house became angry and said to his slave, 'Go out at once into the streets and lanes of the town and bring in the poor, the crippled, the blind, and the lame.' And the slave

said, 'Sir, what you ordered has been done, and there is still room.' Then
the master said to the slave, 'Go out into the roads and lanes, and compel
people to come in, so that my house may be filled. For I tell you, none of
those who were invited will taste my dinner.'"

LUKE 14:16–24

There's so much to be said about this parable. Most commentators agree
that these excuses are pretty weak.[26] Buying a field this large, purchasing
five pairs of oxen, or getting married aren't events that would have suddenly
arisen in the time between the original invitation to the dinner and when
the slave announced it was ready. The host is indignant because such implau-
sible excuses are a deliberate insult to his hospitality.[27] But in his anger, he
doesn't attempt to get his honor back by inviting more people from the same
social status. No, he rejects the model based on reciprocity and extends the
guest list. He chooses to replace his anger with grace. He sends his slave
out to "the streets and lanes" where the people of lower status lived. Even
when the poor, the crippled, the blind, and the lame—you remember, the
ones that Jesus told the Pharisee to invite to the banquet in the conversation
before this one—even when they come, the slave proclaims, "There is still
room" (v. 22).

"There is still room." That's such a stunning line. Whether we view
this table as a metaphor for God's table[28] or as a teaching to expand our
own tables—or, better yet, we embrace both layers of meaning—the point
stands: There's still room at the table. There's room at God's table, so there
should be room at our table. God keeps inviting more people, not to distinct,
sorted tables but to his table. This teaching, just like the earlier one, is also
rooted in God's character. Jesus' vision of a bigger, more inclusive lunchroom is rooted in who God is. He is a God who says, "There is still room
at my table." His desire is for his table to be filled, and our desire should
reflect this also. We compel people to the table because God wants as many
people as possible to respond to his invitation. This is a new social order, a
different kind of lunchroom, where the boundaries that normally exclude
people no longer have value. The list of those invited in the kingdom of God
is unlimited.

In Pursuit of a Full Table

As we saw earlier in this chapter, Jesus didn't just talk about filling the table; he lived it.[29] He wanted tax collectors and sinners at the table. He wanted the religious leaders at the table. And when we look at Jesus' closest community in the Gospels, his twelve disciples, we see that it was far from a homogenous group. The Twelve included a tax collector, who was viewed as traitorous to the Jews for working for the Romans. And it included a zealot,[30] which was an anti-Roman rebel of sorts. Let's just say these two had very different political views on the role of the government and taxes, and yet Jesus wanted them at the same table. Throw in some fishermen, some competitive brothers with a helicopter mom, and you've got quite a diverse group (and that doesn't even begin to account for the larger group of hundreds of disciples who followed Jesus, including a woman whose husband worked for King Herod! [Luke 8:1–3]).

This wasn't diversity just for the sake of diversity. This was honoring the heart of God, which we're told in Luke 15 looks like a shepherd leaving ninety-nine sheep to find the lost one; like a woman turning her house upside down to find a lost coin; and like a father who keeps peering off into the distance hoping his lost son will come home to feast at his table, regardless of what he did or how long he was gone—a father who is also as committed to compelling his other son to stay for dinner because he "wants all the kids at the table, whether they've been lost and distant or faithfully present their entire lives."[31]

God desires a full table. He wants all to belong.

And yet, Luke 14 tells us, there are some who have to be compelled to come to the table. Did you catch that? After the slave invited the poor and blind, he told the master there was still room. And then the master told him to go out even further and "compel" people to come in so that his house would be filled (v. 23). Some commentators read this in light of the social dynamics of reciprocity that we talked about earlier—that basically those who were so far out on the margins wouldn't initially think they could come because they couldn't repay the host. That makes sense to us.

And we worry that those who need to be compelled have a fundamental misunderstanding of the host, incorrectly believing they are being invited to a lunchroom rooted in Genesis 3, not John 17. They don't understand that the host has rejected the current rules of the lunchroom. They don't understand he has thrown the socially acceptable invite list in the trash. They don't understand that he has a never-ending line of chairs to pull up for anyone who wants to come, whether they're early or late, dressed well or not, sinner, tax collector, Pharisee, zealot, or fisherman.

But it wasn't just the characters in the parable or the Pharisees listening to the parable who didn't fully understand the host's actions. The disciples misunderstood, too. Earlier, when Jesus tried to sit at the Samaritans' "table" but was snubbed, James and John wanted to retaliate: "Lord, do you want us to command fire to come down from heaven and consume them?" (Luke 9:54). With their egos bruised because their leader wasn't welcomed, these disciples basically offered to beat someone up in the hallway between classes. They didn't understand that this vision of a new lunchroom was much bigger than they imagined. (Spoiler alert: In Acts 8, John actually goes to the Samaritans' "table," where it seems he not only understands the vision but even helps make it a reality.)

Of course, we, too, often misunderstand the host. We cross people off his invitation list; we communicate that the table is only for some; we opt for the more comfortable old-order lunchroom that has us sorting ourselves into tables with our friends, family, and people who can improve our status in the lunchroom. And yet, despite our history of misunderstanding, despite our messing it up more often than we'd like, Jesus' vision for the lunchroom is worth pursuing.

Jesus pursued this vision up until the very end. At the final dinner Jesus ate with his disciples, on that Thursday night before his death, he showed how serious he was. When Jesus prayed that prayer for oneness, he did so at a table with both Peter and Judas—table companions who would soon deny and betray him. This table isn't just for friends. It's not just for those whose company we enjoy. It's not just for people who have the same professions as us or make the same amount of money we do. It's not just for people who share our political views. It's not just for people we approve of. It's not just for those who have proven themselves trustworthy. It's not just for those who have been responsible religious folks their whole lives or even just for those who are responsible religious folks now. It's not just for those who can clean up their lives really quickly. It's for all who will come to the table because our host ensures there's room for everyone.

Yes, And

The thing about improvisation is that it's not about what you say.
It's listening to what other people say. It's about what you hear.
PAUL MERTON

But one of the things I learned from improvising is that all
of life is an improvisation, whether you like it or not.
ALAN ARKIN

In any ordinary high school lunchroom, there's always the table that, twice a year, doubles as a box office. You know the table—the one where the theater kids sit. Those overly dramatic Broadway wannabes who are just one measure of "Don't Stop Believin'" away from performing a full-scale musical number from *Glee* while you finish eating your tater tots. The table that every fall and spring transforms into the place where teenage thespians beg you to buy a ticket for their mediocre performances as if their very lives depend upon your attendance.

We have always admired the craft of acting and the actors themselves; the ability to convincingly portray a diverse set of characters, to physically and emotionally become someone else, and to have the capacity to memorize huge swaths of lines impresses us to no end. How did Jim Carrey steal Christmas as the Grinch, get birthed from a rhino as Ace Ventura, *and* portray forlorn Joel Barish in *Eternal Sunshine of the Spotless Mind*? How did Chadwick Boseman play both Thurgood Marshall *and* the Black Panther (and within one year of each other!)? How did Meryl Streep sing the songs of Abba in *Mama Mia*, cook like Julia Child in *Julia & Julia, and* run a Catholic school as the extremely stern Sister Aloysius in *Doubt*?

My (Heather's) acting career began and ended on the same day with the singular performance of the fourth-grade class musical, "Santa's Holiday Hoedown," at Van Buren Elementary School in 1994. Although I can't even remember what character I played, I can to this day still sing the chorus of the toe-tappin' opening tune "Goin' to Branson." Why was my time in the spotlight so fleeting? A generous explanation is that I peaked in fourth grade, and there was no reason to continue—how could anything top that country music jamboree, complete with homemade costumes and performed in what was lovingly referred to as the "old gym"? But the more likely reason my acting career began and ended on the same day is that although I did indeed peak in fourth grade, that peak was so low (perhaps more accurately dubbed a "valley") that the honest adults in my life saw they should probably redirect my tone-deaf voice and wooden recitation of lines to somewhere that, well, didn't require singing or acting.

I think part of why I appreciate acting so much is because I'm not good at it. I recognize that the best actors are a rare combination of innate ability and intense devotion to their craft. Did you know that Natalie Portman trained in ballet for over a year—up to eight hours a day, six days a week—to prepare for her role in the 2010 movie *Black Swan*, along with supplemental swim classes and cross-training?[1] Daniel Day-Lewis, preparing to play Hawkeye in the 1992 movie *The Last of the Mohicans*, actually "learned to track and skin animals, build canoes, fight with tomahawks, [and] fire and reload a 12-pound flintlock on the run." And because a hunter in the wild would never be without their gun, apparently Day-Lewis took the gun everywhere, even to Christmas dinner![2]

Following Another's Lead

Of all the types of acting skills, improv impresses me the most, precisely because of an actor's inability to fully prepare, or really prepare at all, for the role ahead of time. Improv, short for improvisation, is the type of live acting where every part of the performance is made up on the spot. Sure, the principles of improv can be learned—there are books and theater courses to teach this art form—but at the end of the day, the actor is left with in-the-moment decisions that can't be rehearsed ahead of time. As a tried-and-true over-preparer, I find it hard even to imagine doing this type of acting. (If I attempted, I'd probably end up looking like Michael Scott when he takes improv classes in *The Office*—paralyzed by indecision until I just started shooting finger guns because it would be the only thing I could come up with in the moment.[3]) Just thinking about doing improv stresses me out.

If you're familiar with improv, you know the most foundational rule is summed up in two words: "Yes, and."[4] That is, no matter what other characters in a scene say or do, an actor's job is to agree with it ("Yes") and then build on it ("and"). If Character One says, "Wow, it's a great day for the beach—the waves are perfect for surfing!", Character Two is to say an unspoken "Yes" to the beach scene, perhaps offering to apply sunscreen to Character One or breaking into a rad surfer dude character to continue the plot. Character Two fails to "Yes, and" if they are, say, suddenly singing in an opera in Paris. In other words, improv isn't a free-for-all that allows an actor to do whatever they want. The actor must enter into a story that's already being told. This relates to another principle of improv, which is that *it's all about the group*. Improv doesn't exist to make one person look funny, and it doesn't work if one person tries to make it a solo showcase. It's all about a community with a shared goal, "a group of characters working together to create something that's never happened before."[5]

A vital tool in successful improv is *active listening*. Since there's no script, the actors must follow one another's lead, which can only happen when they pay attention and listen carefully. Another key tool is *practicing the craft*. The more actors practice improv, the better they get. They become more comfortable with the required spontaneity and learn to course-correct when something doesn't go as planned. Although practicing can't prepare actors for the exact scenario they'll face in a scene, it can help them improve on how to develop characters, deliver lines, and think on their feet.

Faithful Improvisation

No, "faithful improvisation" isn't the name of a corny Christian sketch comedy group (although there's always hope). It's the term New Testament scholar N. T. Wright gives for how Christians on this side of the resurrection are supposed to live as we await Jesus' second coming, when all things will be made new.[6] In other words, it's a way of discerning how to make the lunchroom like Jesus envisioned it. This improvisation concept is a part of Wright's larger understanding of Scripture as narrative—a view of Scripture that has been highly influential for us, as this book shows. Wright compares Scripture to a drama, proposing that it consists of five acts—Creation, the Fall, Israel, Jesus, and the Church. The New Testament speaks of a future sixth act (New Creation), which tells us how the drama is supposed to end. We are currently living in the fifth act—the Church—and our task is to figure out how to live well in this act, which began at Jesus' ascension in Acts 1. (To distinguish between the acts of a play and the New Testament book of Acts, we have put acts of a play in small caps with Roman numerals [e.g., ACT IV] and used standard capitalization and numbers for Scripture references [e.g., Acts 4]).

Reflecting on the relationship between the various ACTS, especially how ACTS I through IV inform ACT V, Wright notes that,

> The earlier parts of the story are to be told precisely as the earlier parts of the story. We do not read Genesis 1 and 2 as though the world were still like that; we do not read Genesis 3 as though ignorant of Genesis 12, of Exodus, or indeed of the gospels. Nor do we read the gospels as though we were ignorant of the fact that they are written precisely in order to make the transition from ACT 4 to ACT 5, the ACT in which we are now living and in which we are to make our own unique, unscripted and yet obedient, improvisation. This is how we are to be the church, for the world.[7]

Reread that last part: "Unique, unscripted and yet obedient." In other words, "Yes, and."

Living well in ACT V begins with "Yes." It looks like listening to and affirming what went on in the first four ACTS (Genesis 1 through John 21), as well as what has already happened in ACT V (Acts 1 until the present time). Improv does not get to ignore the story that's occurred before. Wright compares it to actors trying to perform the lost fifth ACT of a Shakespearean play. The first four ACTS developed characters, established the initial plot, and provided the elements for the story being performed. The first four ACTS, he says, are the "authority" for ACT V, but, he explains,

> This "authority" of the first four acts would not consist—could not consist!—in an implicit command that the actors should repeat parts of the earlier play over and over again. It would consist in the fact of an as yet unfinished drama, containing its own impetus and forward movement, which demanded to be concluded in an appropriate manner.[8]

Unlike a lost Shakespearean script, however, the Christian story already has its end written—we know our fractured lunchroom will be healed when all things are restored. This gives further guidance for the actors to continue the story faithfully.

The Beginning of ACT V

The book of Acts is the beginning of ACT V, the beginning of the church's faithful improvisation, the beginning of these new believers' attempts at making the first-century lunchroom more closely resemble Jesus' John 17 vision for his followers "that the world may believe." As such, Acts is a fruitful place to look as we strive to continue that faithful improvisation today. Remember, we can't say "and," without first saying "Yes." And let's not forget the "and" neither creates a new, unrelated story (a Parisian opera instead of surfing on the beach), nor does it just repeat lines from earlier in the story. It actively listens to the story that has unfolded up until this point and strives to build upon that narrative faithfully. It is both obedient ("Yes") and unscripted ("and"). It is "ferociously loyal to what has gone before and cheerfully open about what must come next."[9] As we consider how to live in the lunchroom today, we want to be faithful to how ACT V began nearly two thousand years ago, which is why we will spend the next few chapters looking closely at Jesus' earliest followers in Acts as they learned to live out the story in a world-altering way.

Most English Bibles refer to Acts simply as "Acts." Occasionally the introduction in a study Bible might give its longer title, "The Acts of the Apostles," which is a hat tip to the earliest and most commonly used title for it in the first few centuries of the church.[10] At that time, if you were to go online and search for "Acts of," your results would include "Acts of Peter," "Acts of Andrew," and—our personal favorite—"Acts of Paul and Thecla."[11] Such works were labeled as the "acts" of whoever was considered the hero of the book.

But we must confess that we actually think "Acts of the Apostles" is a misnomer. The apostles are not the heroes of this narrative—God is (or, more specifically, the Holy Spirit is). In an attempt to retitle it more accurately, New Testament scholar Darrell Bock suggests, "The Acts of the Sovereign God through the Lord Messiah Jesus by His Spirit on Behalf of the Way."[12] This may be a more precise title, but let's be honest, it's way too long.

We're a little more partial to theologian Michael Green's fresh take on a moniker for Acts. In his book of the same title, Green refers to Acts as *Thirty Years that Changed the World*. That title aptly describes a narrative that chronicles how, post-resurrection, the world was turned upside down in the space of a generation. He writes,

> Three crucial decades in world history. That is all it took. In the years between AD 33 and 64 a new movement was born. In those thirty years it got sufficient growth and credibility to become the largest religion the world has ever seen and to change the lives of hundreds of millions of people. It has spread into every corner of the globe and has more than two billion putative adherents. It has had an indelible impact on civilization, on culture, on education, on medicine, on freedom, and of course on the lives of countless people worldwide. And the seedbed for all this, the time when it took decisive root, was in these three decades. It all began with a dozen men and a handful of women, and then the Spirit came.[13]

We propose that Acts, which describes a thirty-year movement that changed the world, is the earliest followers' attempt at faithful improvisation. Their stories—successes, failures, and everything in between—help us think through how to push all these lunchroom tables together today. Acts isn't meant to be read as a dogmatic blueprint for how to do church or a script to be memorized and enacted robotically. More than a how-to book delineating steps for conversion or church growth, Acts is first and foremost a *story*—a story of changed perspectives and growing tables; a story of God's people, empowered by God's Spirit, testifying to and attempting to live out Jesus' vision for a new kind of lunchroom; a story that begins by emphatically saying "Yes" to Jesus' vision and commissioning, followed by an "and"—all of which, thankfully, is directed and empowered by God's Spirit. And, as we'll explore more later, Acts is a story that invites *us* in, challenging *us* to imagine how *our* perspectives need to change, how *our* tables need to grow, how *we* might testify to and continue the lunchroom transformation that Jesus and his earliest followers began, and how *we* might continue to participate in this story actively.

Lights, Camera, Action

So, how did this all start? How did Jesus' followers know that it was their time to take center stage? Let's be honest, their track record of understanding what Jesus taught them is not stellar. But he'd been pretty clear, hadn't he? His vision for a different kind of lunchroom looked like unity with God and others (John 17); it looked like pulling up more and more chairs to the table and compelling even those who didn't think they were invited to come (Luke 14). He'd taught the vision. He'd lived the vision. And now he was entrusting them to keep the vision going.

But before he leaves them, Jesus is blatantly clear about the vision one last time. This time the vision—which is actually a commission—comes with a promise: "You will receive power when the Holy Spirit has come upon you, and you will be my witnesses in Jerusalem, in all Judea and Samaria, and to the ends of the earth" (Acts 1:8). Jesus' followers have a job to do, a part to play, and even though he won't be with them in the flesh, he's

leaving them with another Guide to help them with their faithful improvisation. This verse, Acts 1:8, is at the heart of the theology of Acts. Put
simply, Jesus' charge is a worldwide witness empowered by God's Spirit.
It's time for Jesus' followers to move beyond their own tables into yet unex-
plored parts of the lunchroom.

Acts 1:8, which serves as an outline for the entire book of Acts, is a
series of concentric circles that expand geographically as the gospel moves
outward to include more and more tables. Over the next few chapters, we
hope to show you how this commissioning led these early followers of Jesus
to play their part in a movement that would begin in *Jerusalem*, extend to
Judea and Samaria, and then on to the *ends of the earth*. The good news of
Jesus' resurrection means, among other things, that Jesus' John 17 prayer
for oneness and his Luke 14 invitation to all are still alive.

Promise Kept

If you continue to read into Acts, you see that Jesus' promise of power
became a reality in chapter 2 at Pentecost. The early Jesus-followers started
off strong. It would be hard not to when the Spirit-empowerment at
Pentecost was replete with wind and fire, giving them the miraculous ability
to proclaim the gospel in languages they'd never learned.

Perhaps we shouldn't be surprised that such a bold outpouring of
God's Spirit led to Peter's proclamation of the words of the prophet Joel,
who spoke of a time when God would pour out his Spirit on *all flesh*—men,
women, young, old, slaves and free (Acts 2:17–18, quoting Joel 2:28–29).
Joel's vision sounded a lot like Jesus' lunchroom vision. Dense as Peter
could sometimes be, he couldn't deny that what Joel was talking about was
happening in real time, and so he boldly proclaimed Joel's words: "*Everyone*
who calls on the name of the Lord shall be saved" (Acts 2:21, quoting Joel
2:32, emphasis added).

And perhaps we shouldn't be surprised that such a bold outpouring
of God's Spirit led to the formation of a radically inclusive community—a
community that "had all things in common" (Acts 2:44); a community that
"would sell their possessions and goods and distribute the proceeds to all,

as any had need" (Acts 2:45); a community that "spent much time together in the temple ... broke bread at home and ate their food with glad and generous hearts, praising God and having the goodwill of all the people" (Acts 2:46–47).

And perhaps we also shouldn't be surprised that such a bold outpouring of God's Spirit led to thousands coming to believe in Jesus: "That day about three thousand persons were added" (Acts 2:41). Just a few verses later Luke reiterates, "And day by day the Lord added to their number those who were being saved" (Acts 2:47). And again, two chapters later, he updates his readers: "Many of those who heard the word believed, and they numbered about five thousand" (Acts 4:4).

The lunchroom didn't just increase in numbers; it was more than a church-growth movement. Something deeper was happening in Jerusalem. The very nature of the lunchroom was being transformed, as Luke describes repeatedly. Similar to his description in Acts 2, Luke tells of the unity and generosity of the believers in Acts 4:

> Now the whole group of those who believed were of one heart and soul, and no one claimed private ownership of any possessions, but everything they owned was held in common. With great power the apostles gave their testimony to the resurrection of the Lord Jesus, and great grace was upon them all. There was not a needy person among them, for as many as owned lands or houses sold them and brought the proceeds of what was sold. They laid it at the apostles' feet, and it was distributed to each as any had need.
>
> ACTS 4:32–35

In a very short amount of time, this Jesus movement was on its way to changing the world.

And then, of course, they all lived happily ever after ... right?

Mission accomplished.

Class dismissed.

Curtain closed.

Well, not quite.

Up to this point in Acts, the improvisation, the response to the story coming to life around them, was somewhat natural and reflexive. But these early followers still had quite a bit to learn. So far, they had only inhabited one section of the lunchroom. We're not sure they even truly grasped what they were being empowered to accomplish. Sure, Peter had preached that *all* who called on the name of the Lord would be saved, but Jesus didn't just mean *all in Jerusalem*, all in Peter's corner of the lunchroom. Remember the concentric circles laid out in Acts 1:8? Even by Acts 4, the early church hadn't yet approached the idea of moving beyond the "Jerusalem Circle" into the "Judea and Samaria Circle," let alone the "Ends of the Earth Circle." At the end of Acts 7, they were still in Jerusalem. But the stage for the drama was about to grow exponentially. In the words of Bible scholars Gordon Fee and Douglas Stuart, the gospel was about to move "from its Jerusalem-based, Judaism-oriented beginnings to … a worldwide, Gentile-predominant phenomenon."[14]

But this transformation would not be comfortable.

A Crucible

In many ways, Acts—or really, all of ACT V—can be compared to a crucible. In literal terms, the word *crucible* refers to a container where materials are subjected to extremely high temperatures in order to form something new. This means that before change can occur, there must be a challenge or a trial that brings about the interaction of different elements to produce a thing that didn't exist before. Just like the story of Acts, a crucible requires some discomfort to bring something new and better to life. From a literary perspective, the crucible is the place in the narrative where all the different elements of the story thus far interact in such a way that it leads to the creation of something new. That's what's happening in Acts. Living out Jesus' vision will not be easy.

In the next three chapters of this book, we will explore how the early followers of Jesus wrestled with the challenges they faced as they began to explore other parts of the lunchroom and learn how to push the lunchroom tables together. Was God actually calling these earlier followers to share tables with enemies? With religious, ethnic, and sexual "others"? What would it take for the leaders of this movement to obey God's commands when those commands seemed to go against everything they'd ever known and done? In what ways should their sacred Scriptures inform the community on the pressing question of who was allowed to sit at what table?

Aren't their questions about the lunchroom the same questions we have today? As we also try to improvise faithfully in ACT V, aren't we wrestling with what *our* concentric circles are? Who or where is our Jerusalem, our Judea, and our Samaria? Who or where are our ends of the earth?

Some of the questions and proposals in this book may be difficult for some of us. Crucibles always are. This broken lunchroom of a world continues to distort, divide, disconnect, and dehumanize. But Jesus' earliest followers—who themselves were figuring out the art of "Yes, and"—show us that the creation of something new is possible and provide some help and hope for us today as we try to move the plot of ACT V closer to its resolution in ACT VI, which is to say, closer to the realization of Jesus' vision for the lunchroom.

To Those with Their Backs against the Wall

It cannot be denied that too often the weight of the Christian movement has been on the side of the strong and the powerful and against the weak and oppressed—this, despite the gospel.
HOWARD THURMAN

Try your best to make goodness attractive. That's one of the toughest assignments you'll ever be given.
FRED ROGERS

In 1935, the great theologian, educator, and civil rights leader Howard Thurman traveled with university students to India, Burma, and what is now Sri Lanka. Over coffee at the University of Colombo in Sri Lanka, the principal confronted Dr. Thurman: "What are *you* doing over here?" The principal elaborated:

More than three hundred years ago your forefathers were taken from the western coast of Africa as slaves. The people who dealt in the slave traffic were Christians. The name of one of the famous British slave vessels was "Jesus." The men who *bought* the slaves were Christians. Christian ministers, quoting the Christian apostle Paul, gave the sanction of religion to the system of slavery. Some seventy years or more ago you were freed by a man [Abraham Lincoln] who was not a professing Christian, but was rather the spearhead of certain political, social, and economic forces, the significance of which he himself did not understand. During all the period since then you have lived in a Christian nation in which you are segregated, lynched, and burned. Even in the church, I understand, there is segregation. One of my students who went to your country sent me a clipping telling about a Christian church in which the regular Sunday worship was interrupted so that many could join a mob against one of your fellows. When he had been caught and done to death, they came back to resume their worship of their Christian God.

I am a Hindu. I do not understand. Here you are in my country, staying deep within the Christian faith and tradition. I do not wish to seem rude to you. But, sir, I think you are a traitor to all the darker peoples of the earth. I am wondering what you, an intelligent man, can say in defense of your position?[1]

The discussion that followed lasted hours. In light of the history he'd been confronted with, Thurman was forced to grapple with the meaning of his faith in Jesus. His book *Jesus and the Disinherited*, written in 1935 and first published in 1949, emerged from the wrestling prompted by this conversation. Less than a hundred pages in length, this small but mighty work has impacted figures as influential as Dr. Martin Luther King, Jr., who often carried a copy on his many travels.[2]

Thurman, who grew up in America's South and was well aware of the strategic seating arrangements of the lunchroom, begins *Jesus and the Disinherited* like this:

Many and varied are the interpretations dealing with the teachings and life of Jesus of Nazareth. But few of these interpretations deal with what the teachings and the life of Jesus have to say to those who stand, at a moment in human history, with *their back against the wall*. To those who need profound succor and strength to enable them to live in the present with dignity and creativity, Christianity often has been sterile and of little avail.[3]

Why is this the case? Why do so many find themselves with their backs pressed up against the wall? Why have many Christians been content with a lunchroom hierarchy that means that those who are considered "different" or "outsiders" don't have a place at their table? Why is it that Christians today, during Thurman's time, and at so many other points throughout history, have been impotent in dealing with the issues that place people against the wall—whether those issues are race, sexuality, religion, economics, or other such categories? Why do we so readily use these categories to sort people into their separate tables or, worse yet, leave them with no table at all? Thurman provides an answer: "It is the sin of pride and arrogance that has tended to vitiate the missionary impulse and to make of it an instrument of self-righteousness on the one hand and racial superiority on the other."[4]

Is our religion actually good news to "the other," to the disinherited, the dispossessed? What does our faith in Jesus offer to those with their backs against the wall? Thurman's words from the 1930s continue to admonish us today: "The search for an answer to this question is perhaps the most important religious quest of modern life."[5]

Trouble in Paradise

The book of Acts—this narrative detailing thirty years that changed the world—helps us wrestle with Thurman's "most important religious quest." Even as the disciples made real strides at living out Jesus' vision for the lunchroom, there were significant challenges. Deep and consummate change, the kind Jesus called Nicodemus to, isn't easy. For starters, not everyone bought into Jesus' vision—some thought that bringing others to the table meant less room or resources for themselves (Acts 5:1–11). Others thought this vision threatened their own place at the top of the lunchroom food chain (Acts 5:17–33). Beyond that, when you actually invite *all* kinds of people to one lunch table, things tend to get messy. Although Acts 2 and 4 show no one needing anything, Acts 6 reveals that a particularly vulnerable group had been pushed away from the table—a group of Greek-speaking widows who did not understand the Aramaic language spoken by most of the earliest followers in Jerusalem. As women immersed in a patriarchal world, reliant on others for daily food, and easily misunderstood due to cultural barriers, their vulnerabilities were reminiscent of Hagar's. Depending on how you translate *paratheoreo* in Acts 6:1, these widows were at best "overlooked" (NASB, NIV), lost in the shuffle of the new lunchroom; at worst they were "neglected" (NRSV, ESV) or even "discriminated against" (NLT). Changing the dynamics of the lunchroom isn't easy.

Fortunately, when the Hellenists (the Greek-speaking Jewish Christians) brought this problem to the attention of the Hebrews (the Aramaic-speaking Jewish Christians), they incorporated the laws of improv: They listened and responded with a "Yes, and." As a community, they took the "Yes" principles of including all at the table and worked together to discern the "and" for this particular scenario, allocating seven Greek-speaking Jews to care for the widows. They took seriously the testimony of those who had been relegated to the margins of the lunchroom (whether intentionally or not), and they invited and empowered people who were best able to meet the needs of that marginalized community (i.e., fellow Greek speakers) to ensure that everyone had a place at the table.

This story is one of the first divisions narrated in Acts, but it's definitely not the last. Living out Jesus' lunchroom vision was going to take practice. Although the church was doing pretty well with the "witness" part of Acts 1:8, they still had work to do on the "worldwide" part. As we mentioned earlier, Jesus wanted them to be witnesses not just in Jerusalem (which they began to do in Acts 2–7) but also in Judea (the region around Jerusalem), Samaria (the region north of Judea), and to the ends of the earth (everywhere else). The vision was bigger. The lunchroom was bigger. They would need to learn how to push many more tables together.

Even . . . Them?

Before we get any further into the Acts narrative, we should note that hostility toward the early church had been escalating. It began in Acts 4 with an overnight imprisonment for Peter and John. In Acts 5, it intensifies to more imprisonment plus an added flogging. The martyrdom of the first Jesus-follower takes place in Acts 7, and eventually culminates in a full-blown "severe persecution" in Acts 8 that leads to all but the apostles being scattered outside of Jerusalem into Judea and Samaria (not-so-coincidentally aligning with where Jesus told them to testify in Acts 1:8). For any of you familiar with the game of pool or billiards, imagine the very first shot, the break shot, where all the balls are gathered and racked up, and the cue ball is hit so hard that the others scatter all over the table. That's what happens in Acts 8. In this break-shot moment, those once gathered in Jerusalem are now scattered into the surrounding areas. But rather than letting the scattering slow them down, these early Christians use it as an opportunity to pull up more chairs to the lunchroom table.

The first two stories after this break-shot moment center on a man named Philip. He was one of the seven Greek-speaking Jews who had been appointed to care for the widows, and Luke describes him as "a man full of faith and the Holy Spirit" (Acts 6:5). The Spirit continued to empower the early church to live out Jesus' vision, but we also believe that the improvisation practice Philip had with the widow situation helped equip him for his next lunchroom assignments, both of which come in Acts 8.

Continuing to say, "Yes, and," Philip travels to Samaria. The geographical and cultural setting of this story is crucial for our understanding of how Philip navigates the lunchroom. As we explained in chapter three, the Samaritans' history was contested, going back hundreds of years before Jesus. Their own claim was that they, not the Jews, worshiped Yahweh in accordance with the most ancient Israelite traditions. Jews in the time of Jesus, however, begged to differ. According to 2 Kings 17, the Assyrians came to colonize Samaria after they defeated Israel. They populated the towns of Samaria with pagans, and when those settlers were killed by lions because they didn't know how to properly worship Yahweh (seriously—go read 2 Kings!), the Assyrians had an Israelite priest come to teach them how to worship the God of Israel. The inhabitants of Samaria then accepted the Israelite religion *alongside* their former religious practices. Thus—and here's the important part—Jews viewed Samaritans as syncretistic both ethnically (in that they married people of other nations) and religiously (in that they combined tenets of Judaism with foreign religions).[6]

The divide between Jews and Samaritans went far deeper than the theological disagreements that separate us today, such as those between Baptists and Methodists, Calvinists and Arminians, complementarians and egalitarians, and so forth. It was more than a dispute in which one person cancels another on social media. We're talking about violence and desecration rooted in different religious beliefs, different worship spaces, different sets of Scripture, and competing understandings of who the true people of God were.[7] These groups were intense rivals. They were enemies.[8] In Luke 9:51–56—after the Samaritans rejected Jesus—James and John asked Jesus if he wanted them to call down fire on the Samaritans. (The answer was no, followed by an indicting parable shortly after in Luke 10:25–37 about a *good* Samaritan because Jesus wasn't playing their games.) Not coincidentally, the disciples never asked for consuming fire when any other group rejected Jesus. The prejudice was real, and it was strong, and we miss the power of Acts 8 if we don't get that. In traveling to Samaria, Philip is going to have to recognize that God wants even his rivals to have a seat at the table.

The Samaritans welcome Philip and listen to his message, and many are baptized. So far so good. But then word of the Samaritans' conversions makes its way back to the apostles in Jerusalem. Surely Peter—the one who preached about *all flesh* receiving God's Spirit—and John—the one whom Jesus rebuked when he offered to call down fire on Samaritans—would rejoice at this good news! Surely!

Surely?

Well, not exactly.

When the apostles in Jerusalem get word of what happened in Samaria, they send Peter and John to check it out (Acts 8:14). Upon arrival, they pray for the Samaritans, "that they might receive the Holy Spirit (for as yet the Spirit had not come upon any of them; they had only been baptized in the name of the Lord Jesus)" (Acts 8:15–16). Back in Acts 2, as well as in several other places in Acts, receiving the Holy Spirit is connected with baptism, so what's going on here? Why hadn't the Holy Spirit shown up? We think it's because Peter and John needed to see it for themselves. They needed to embrace their enemies, to touch them. They needed to witness—*even be a part of*—God pouring his Spirit on the Samaritans—as he had promised to do on *all flesh.*[9]

This story, then, isn't just about the lunchroom table getting bigger to include the Samaritans, though that's certainly a part of it. It's also about practicing faithful improvisation, in so much as when Peter and John say "Yes, and" to Jesus' vision for the lunchroom, even ethnic and religious rivals are invited to the table. Maybe God actually meant what he said through the prophet Joel—that *all* who call on the name of the Lord would be saved. God wants *all* to have a seat at his table. And "all" really does mean *all.*

Opening Our Insides

One of the reasons some kids hate school lunchtime is because their lunches just aren't as cool as other kids' lunches. Now, you may be thinking, "How can a lunch be cool?" Food is food, right?

Wrong.

In the lunchroom food hierarchy, a build-your-own-pizza Lunchable is *objectively cooler* than a bologna and cheese sandwich your mom made. Prepackaged Doritos in a colorful bag advertising just how *blazin' hot* each chip is are *objectively cooler* than Kroger-brand pretzels hastily crammed in a fold-over baggie. A cold can of Strawberry Passion Awareness Fruitopia[10] straight out of the vending machine is *objectively cooler* than a room-temperature Hi-C fruit punch juice box. None of this is up for debate. Ask any kid in the lunchroom.

I (Heather) will let you guess which kind of lunches I had growing up. I'm not bitter. Really, I'm not.

"Why can't you just buy *cool* food like a *cool* mom?"[11] I would plead with my undeterred mother, only to receive a breakdown of the cost differences between bag-your-own pretzels and prepackaged Doritos and a math lesson in how "fifty cents[12] a day at the vending machine is more than twice as much as buying a ten-pack of juice boxes for $1.99!" Cue the overly dramatic sigh of a typical teenager.

My mom just didn't understand that the contents of my lunch were more than just physical sustenance. They were social currency. Once we'd all squeezed around the lunchroom table, everyone would compare the contents of their lunchboxes, and then the bartering would begin. "I'll give you my Fruit by the Foot if you give me one of your Fudge Rounds!" "Wanna swap your Oreos for my Dunkaroos?" My problem was, of course, that no one wanted a homemade bologna and cheese sandwich. I didn't stand a chance at getting a Lunchable. I couldn't even convince someone that my sandwich was worth their string cheese. The best I might have to offer was generic brand fruit snacks. (I'm not talking about Fruit Smiles. Those things are delicious. I'm talking weird Aldi-brand "Lunch Buddies" or something like that.) *The contents mattered.*

Anne Lamott says it like this:

> Here is the main thing I know about public school lunches: it only *looked* like a bunch of kids eating lunch. It was really about opening our insides in front of everyone…. *The contents of your lunch said whether or not you and your family were Okay. Some bag lunches, like some people, were Okay, and some weren't.* There was a code, a right and acceptable way. It was that simple.[13]

The Kid Who Wasn't "Okay"

In Acts 8, Philip's next lunchroom assignment was to join the table of the kid who wasn't "okay," the kid who, kind of like Hagar, had his back against the wall. In this narrative, God is clearly orchestrating their meeting, as Philip receives directions from an angel to go to a remote part of the lunchroom—what Luke describes as "a wilderness road" (Acts 8:26). On this wilderness road, the Holy Spirit directs Philip to join this man in his chariot (Acts 8:29). Philip says yes, and *runs* to the chariot (Acts 8:30). As theologian Willie James Jennings puts it, "God is chasing after [him]."[14] The host wants his table full.

Like Hagar, this character who wasn't "okay" is complex. Parts of him were quite socially acceptable. Honorable, even. But other parts … well, not so much. We don't know this man's name (isn't that often the case for those with their backs against the wall?), but we do know quite a few things about him.

We know he's religious. We'd even call him devout, considering he'd made a pilgrimage all the way from Ethiopia to Jerusalem to worship the God of Israel.

We know his job. He's a court official over the queen of Ethiopia's treasury. And apparently his paycheck came with enough wealth to travel in a chariot (the BMW of the ancient world), own a scroll of Isaiah (it was not common for individuals to own scrolls, especially not of a long book like Isaiah), and be literate enough to read that scroll.

We know he's from Ethiopia, which means he's a foreigner. For most people in the ancient world, Ethiopia was considered a really far-off land. Many may have even viewed it as "the ends of the earth," signifying again the fulfillment of Jesus' command to be his witnesses to the ends of the earth (Acts 1:8).

So why is this guy's back against the wall? He sounds like someone a lot of people would want to sit at their table.

Well, there's one other detail about this guy that puts him squarely in the "not okay" category. And this detail is key for Luke, given it's his primary descriptor of the man.[15]

This man is a eunuch.

To most people today, this descriptor is kind of ... weird. When did you last use the word "eunuch" in a conversation? Have you ever talked about a eunuch besides when referring to this Bible character? "Eunuch" just isn't a category we use.

However, "eunuch" *was* a significant category in the ancient world.[16] To state it bluntly, a eunuch is a man who has been castrated or born without all his sexual anatomy intact. In the Roman Empire, eunuchs were most often found as priests serving the Great Mother Goddess, as slaves in imperial or aristocratic households (because they couldn't produce illegitimate heirs), or as exotic sex slaves.[17] Depending on when and how the castration was done, most eunuchs wouldn't develop like typical men because their mutilated bodies wouldn't produce hormones like a typical male.[18] They were, as Jennings describes it, "neither unambiguously male nor female."[19] Perhaps surprisingly, both Greco-Roman and Jewish sources tell us a good bit about what they thought of eunuchs, and, perhaps unsurprisingly, it's not pretty. They were stereotyped as immoral and monstrous. Josephus, a Jewish writer and contemporary of Luke, likens eunuchs to child killers (since they can't procreate) and tells his readers to shun them and flee all dealings with them.[20] In a society where honor was tied to gender, eunuchs were viewed suspiciously because they were seen as sexually ambiguous.

What's the problem with this ambiguity? Well, the Pentateuch's concern with holiness included maintaining purity through distinct boundaries, ensuring the separation of different categories. Leviticus 19:19, for example, forbids mixing different animals, seeds, and fabrics: "You shall not let your animals breed with a different kind; you shall not sow your field with two kinds of seed; nor shall you put on a garment made of two different materials." Perhaps we shouldn't be surprised, then, that eunuchs are forbidden from fully participating in the assembly of God's people (Deut. 23:1), whether because they appeared to be a mix of the male-female category or because they weren't considered whole. To be sure, Israel's Scriptures contained a vision of a time when eunuchs would be welcome in the temple, but that was a vision for the *future*, the age to come when God would set all things right (Isa. 56:4–6).

There's a sense of sad irony permeating this man's story. Despite his devotion to God, his countries-long pilgrimage may have still culminated in him being relegated to the temple's outermost courts. And his senior role in the treasury, with the wealth and literacy that came with it, was rooted in his socially ostracized status as a eunuch because it secured the trust necessary for him to serve the queen.

New Testament scholar Mikeal Parsons describes it like this:

Crossing socioeconomic borders between the elite and the outcast only made the eunuch that much more of a liminal figure—trusted, yet treated with suspicion; prosperous, yet ostracized; the "powerful" whose access to power, ironically, came only through his humiliation (cf. Luke 1:48). It is this kind of person whom Philip is directed by the Spirit to approach (8:29)—a social outcast, living on the liminal in terms of his sexual identity, his religious identification, and his socioeconomic status.[21]

His story reminds us that the stories of those with their backs against the wall are often more complex than they seem. Yet Philip doesn't need to resolve this complexity before he can engage the eunuch—God's clear directions to Philip via an angel (Acts 8:26) and the Holy Spirit (Acts 8:29) signal that Philip is supposed to join this man's table.

Finding Himself in the Story

When Philip approaches this eunuch, he finds him reading Isaiah 53:7–8, which, as Luke records, says this: "Like a sheep he was led to the slaughter, and like a lamb silent before its shearer, so he does not open his mouth. In his humiliation justice was denied him. Who can describe his generation? For his life is taken away from the earth." This is known as one of the "Suffering Servant" passages, where Isaiah announces the suffering and eventual exaltation of the servant of the Lord. Early Christians naturally identified this servant with Jesus.[22]

But this eunuch didn't know who Jesus was. We suspect he was reading Isaiah 53 because it sounded like his own story.[23] Aren't we all drawn to those Scriptures that resonate with important parts of our story? Read it again through the eyes of a eunuch: "Like a sheep he was *led to the slaughter*, and like a lamb silent *before its shearer*, so he does not open his mouth. In his *humiliation justice was denied him*. Who can describe his *generation*? For his life is taken away from the earth." When the eunuch asks Philip if Isaiah was writing autobiographically or if Isaiah was referring to someone else, perhaps it's because the eunuch wonders if that "someone else" was like him, someone he could relate to. Philip tells the eunuch that Isaiah 53 is about another servant, Jesus, who understood the humiliation and injustice the eunuch experienced but who received vindication in the end. Like the eunuch, Jesus knew what it was to have his back against the wall, but Jesus' story shows the eunuch that he doesn't have to stay there.

When Luke says, "Philip began to speak, and starting with this scripture he proclaimed to him the good news about Jesus" (Acts 8:35), many of us imagine that Philip whipped out his pocket-sized New Testament and started reading to him from one of the Gospels. But, of course, the

New Testament wasn't written then. What Philip *does* have is a scroll of Isaiah (okay, and some lessons from widows and Samaritans, some guidance from the Holy Spirit, and a burgeoning understanding of faithful improvisation). Perhaps he just rolled the scroll over to Isaiah 56,[24] which was a prophecy about a coming day of salvation and deliverance in which the eunuch and the foreigner—both of which describe this man and were the basis of his exclusion per Deuteronomy 23—would be able to participate in the assembly of God's people fully. Old Testament scholar Paul Hanson describes the significance of Isaiah's vision like this: "As emphatic as was the exclusion in the Deuteronomic law ('even to the tenth generation'), so emphatic is the inclusion here: 'Their [the foreigners'] burnt offerings and their sacrifices will be accepted on my altar' (v. 7)."[25] So, too, is the emphasis on the inclusion of eunuchs, whom God will give "an everlasting name that shall not be cut off" (Isa. 56:5). Isaiah envisioned a time when God would bring deliverance, justice, and salvation *for all*. And just as Peter, reading the prophet Joel at Pentecost, declared that God pouring out his Spirit upon all flesh was happening *now* (Acts 2:17–18), Philip, too, interprets the eunuch's story in light of the cross and resurrection; an existence of pain and exclusion becomes a story of redemption and restoration and hope. He didn't have to wait for the end times to be welcomed to the table among God's people. Philip was pulling up a chair *now*.

When the eunuch hears this good news, he asks, "What is to prevent me from being baptized?" (Acts 8:36). We used to read that question in a tone of great anticipation, assuming that the implied answer was a resounding, "Nothing prevents you!" But after understanding the eunuch's story, which included his fair share of exclusion from most lunch tables, we suspect his tone was more guarded—something more along the lines of, "What's the catch?"[26] But there is no catch. Philip stops the chariot and immediately baptizes the man. The Spirit then mysteriously snatches Philip away, leaving the man headed back to Ethiopia, the ends of the earth, rejoicing. Jesus' vision is coming to fruition. His followers are empowered by God's Spirit and find themselves—ready or not—learning their roles in ACT V.

Climb in the Chariot

Philip climbed in the chariot with a kid whose back was against the wall. We believe we're called to faithfully improvise our part in the story and do the same. The categories may be different today, or they may be strikingly similar. Because, let's be honest, the world in which we live is still one big lunchroom with the contents of each person's lunch indicating whether each of us is "okay" or not. Some lunches, like some people, are considered "okay," and some, for various reasons, are deemed "not okay." As Lamott said, there is "a code [in the lunchroom], a right and acceptable way," though often that code is unspoken and inconsistent. We reduce people to their body size, their relationship status, their age, their race, their disability, their legal status, their sexuality, their place of origin, their socioeconomic status. And in doing so, we reduce our lives and each other's. When we do this—and we *always* do this—there is inevitably a person or persons left with their back against the wall. Who those people are varies depending on what categories are most valuable at each of our tables, but we are absolutely convinced that Jesus is going to seek out the ones whose backs are against the wall.

And he's not just with them; he's *for* them. When teaching his disciples, Jesus lifted up eunuchs as models for life in his kingdom (Matt. 19:12). He also lifted up widows (Luke 21:1–4), the poor (Luke 6:20), the depressed (Matt. 5:4), and a whole host of others with their backs against the wall. These people aren't just *allowed* or *tolerated* at the table. They're not welcomed begrudgingly. Those with their backs against the wall have something to teach others at the table, at least in part because of how their stories are interwoven with the story of Jesus.

Who has their back against the wall today? Who has been "denied justice" or "humiliated"? Who has been viewed as less valuable? The elderly or the immigrant? The single (or the single *again*)? The formerly incarcerated, those struggling with mental illness, or the person speaking broken English? The neurodivergent or the chronically ill? The person whose self-descriptor we just don't quite understand (or, honestly, don't want to understand)? How might their stories of hurt, exclusion, and alienation be understood in light of Jesus' story, regardless of the contents of their lunch?

For us to faithfully improvise might be as simple as climbing up in the chariot and helping someone find their place in the story.

A Voice Crying in the Wilderness

In a world where kids (and adults) love superheroes with powers from shapeshifting to invisibility, teleportation to clairvoyance, super strength to super speed, it's surprising how popular a man in a cardigan wielding a tiger puppet named Daniel could become. That hero, of course, is the one and only Fred Rogers.

Mister Rogers hosted a children's television program, *Mister Rogers' Neighborhood*, for thirty-three years before his passing two decades ago. He ventured into children's television because the first time he watched kids' programming, he hated it. "[It] was such demeaning behavior," he remarked. "And if there's anything that bothers me, it's one person demeaning another."[27] He vowed to use the medium to make the world a better place.

More philosopher than entertainer, Mister Rogers led a renaissance of kindness and understanding. One might even describe him as a voice crying in the wilderness. We think the moniker "prophet" quite nicely fits this ordained Presbyterian minister who, in 1969, took on the government in Washington, DC, when public television funds were threatened. Expressing his belief in the transformative power of children's television to instill hope and cultivate more productive citizens, his impassioned speech convinced and captivated even the most skeptical politicians. As a result, instead of cutting funding for public television, they actually increased it from nine million to twenty-two million dollars.[28]

In the past five or so years, following two movies documenting the impact of his life,[29] Mister Rogers found his way back into the conversation, just as polarization at US lunch tables hit some all-time highs. Nicholas Ma—one of the producers of the documentary *Won't You Be My Neighbor?*—spoke about the influence of Mister Rogers in our world:

> Fred wasn't a superhero, and his goal wasn't to show us that he was powerful or that he could singlehandedly save us from whatever problems confronted us…. He called us to see one another in our fullest

humanity—to reach beyond the categories and divisions that estrange us from each other. And he urged us to be proud of our uniqueness, to believe in our own inherent worthiness and to understand that others are inherently worthy too.[30]

In calling us to "see one another in our fullest humanity," Mister Rogers did the simplest things in profound, paradigm-shifting ways. In the 1960s, for example, when racial tensions in the States were at a fever pitch, Mister Rogers performed the equivalent of climbing up in the chariot of a eunuch.

During this era, one particularly ugly manifestation of segregation was the scheduling of separate swimming times for Black and white children at public pools. What should have been an act of fun and refreshment some-times devolved into heated conflicts. In one of the most horrific incidents, a man in St. Augustine, Florida, poured acid into a pool occupied by Black children that had been designated "whites only."[31]

Mister Rogers responded to incidents like these in a manner that only someone who taught children how to see one another in their fullest humanity could. On May 9, 1969, Fred Rogers sent a very deliberate message during an episode of *Mister Rogers' Neighborhood*.[32] The show concluded with Mister Rogers sitting beside an inflatable pool filled with water. He told the audience that it had been a very hot day, and he had decided to soak his feet in this small pool. As he did so, a regular character on the show, Officer Clemmons—a Black police officer played by François Clemmons—came on the screen. Mister Rogers invited him to join him by putting his feet in the pool. Officer Clemmons removed his shoes and socks and rested his feet in the same pool as Mister Rogers. And in the simplest of gestures, his viewers were invited to see the world differently. No fanfare, no political statements. Just Fred Rogers living out how to see one another in our fullest humanity.

Years later, during Officer Clemmons's final appearance on the show, he and Mister Rogers recreated the pool scene.[33] As the episode closed, Mister Rogers and Officer Clemmons both took their feet out of the water. And as naturally and instinctually as we imagine Jesus did throughout his ministry, Mister Rogers took a towel, knelt down, and helped dry the feet of Officer Clemmons. In his own way, amid a broken and fractured society, with this simple gesture, Mister Rogers attempted to show his viewers how to see each other differently and brought Isaiah 56 one step closer to fulfillment:

> For thus says the LORD:
> To the eunuchs who keep my Sabbaths,
> who choose the things that please me
> and hold fast my covenant,
> I will give, in my house and within my walls,
> a monument and a name
> better than sons and daughters;
> I will give them an everlasting name
> that shall not be cut off.
> And the foreigners who join themselves to the LORD,
> to minister to him, to love the name of the LORD,
> and to be his servants,
> all who keep the Sabbath and do not profane it
> and hold fast my covenant—
> these I will bring to my holy mountain
> and make them joyful in my house of prayer;
> their burnt offerings and their sacrifices
> will be accepted on my altar,
> for my house shall be called a house of prayer
> for all peoples.
>
> ISAIAH 56:4–7

Look Who's Coming to Dinner

Sometimes it takes an act of God to convince us that deeply established assumptions about God and our world suddenly have to change.
MATTHEW SKINNER

It's the things you learn after you know it all that count.
COACH JOHN WOODEN

In the history of learning, it is only a slight exaggeration to say that I (Mark) easily rank in the top tier of the slowest learners of all time. (I do realize there are no actual rankings in this life category, previous or current, to verify that truth. You'll just have to take my word for it or ask to see my college transcripts.) After almost six decades of life, I have become acutely aware that it just takes me longer to grasp ideas and behaviors.

The primary reason for my tortoise-like learning pace has less to do with my cognitive capabilities and more to do with my not always being ready to learn, unlearn, and relearn. My struggle to grasp the rationale behind a new idea, combined with a deficiency in the relevant social and practical skills to process and comprehend principles, concepts, and ideologies, determines the speed of my learning. This has not only affected my academic endeavors but also my vocation, marriage, fatherhood, and even how I neighbor. I would love to be a fast learner—able to make sense of and discern the deeper things of life at a much quicker pace—and I have often found myself uttering phrases like, "I wish I had understood [*insert idea or concept here*] much sooner; my life and the world around me would have improved significantly."

The good news is that once I do come to some understanding of an idea or belief, I embed that son of a gun deep within my being. Once I *have it*, there is very little chance it will ever leave. When I finally grasp a truth, when I am able to comprehend, embody, and enflesh a particular idea, life-long transformation usually follows. It takes me a while, but once change comes, there is no going back.

In view of what I've shared above, one might assume that some people simply learn things faster than others, that for some, their DNA makes it easier to gain understanding, and we just have to live with the lot we've been given. But the research doesn't seem to support those assumptions. While attempting to identify the unique characteristics that contribute to some persons learning faster than others, cognitive scientist and education researcher Paulo Carvalho concludes the following: "After looking at nearly 7,000 students using different kinds of educational technology (such as online courses and educational games) in more than 1.3 million interactions, we were dumbfounded to find that students learn at surprisingly similar rates. There are no such things as fast and slow learners!"[1] (This is evidently something else for me to learn.) Carvalho continues,

> Students master concepts through opportunities to practice them. They start at different levels of proficiency but, when provided with high-quality practice opportunities, learn at about the same speed. Yes, they will end in different places—but that's because they have different starting lines, not because they are quicker or slower to learn. *That means the types of opportunities you get matter.*[2]

We believe that the opportunities to learn a different way of living in the lunchroom are vast and innumerable. None of us lack moments in life when we can ask different questions and respond in different ways and, in turn, produce different results in this fractured world. As we maneuver in and out of the different pockets of other people's lives, we have ample chances to embody something more akin to the ways of Jesus. We hope the previous chapters have effectively highlighted that we cannot dismiss the brokenness of our world, nor can we sidestep the words of Jesus to participate in a lunchroom redesign if we want to take following him seriously. Therefore, a key question remains: Do we truly grasp that a deep, consummate paradigm shift is possible, regardless of how well or fast we learn? Are we prepared to consider a change in mindset and behavior, believing the truth of this simple statement: It's never too late to be what you might become?[3]

More Messy Scribble than Tidy Arc

If you're a fan of good storytelling, you know that the best characters in the best stories undergo a significant transformation. When viewed in the flow of the story, this transformation will look like an arc or trajectory. That is also true of the stories that each of us live individually. Our personal and communal lives tell stories—whether we want them to or not—and these stories ebb and flow as we learn, unlearn, and relearn in our everyday experiences.

In the storyline of Scripture, Peter's trajectory is one of the most fascinating to trace. From his first encounter with Jesus on the shore of the Sea of Galilee after a miraculous catch of fish to becoming part of Jesus' inner circle to declaring Jesus as the Christ—Peter proved himself loyal and faithful.[4] Yet, Peter's growth trajectory didn't always trend upward. Jesus' responses to Peter included, "Get behind me, Satan," "You of little faith," and "Why are you holding a bloody ear? Put that sword away!" (Okay, we made that last one a little more colorful than the Gospel accounts.)[5] Peter was not known for his consistent and unswerving personality. He was impulsive, cautious, brave, cowardly, strong, and weak.

Peter's story includes a campfire scene, where, shortly after denying Jesus for a third time, the rooster crows, and he locks eyes with his Lord. Devastated by his betrayal, Peter leaves and weeps bitterly.[6] Though he was *last* to the empty tomb when he and the Beloved Disciple raced there (an odd detail that John gives us about Peter's running prowess), later that day Peter, alongside the other disciples, was among the *first* to see the risen Jesus.[7] And we read in the last chapter of John that Peter was given another opportunity, post-resurrection, at the very same Sea of Galilee where it all started, to answer another three questions.[8] Around another campfire, after another surprising haul of fish, Jesus generously and graciously gave Peter a different memory that would outlast his campfire denials.

Peter's trajectory looks more like a messy scribble than a tidy arc, and this unpredictable and sometimes erratic journey continues into Acts with a commission to testify to the ends of the earth and with the giving of the Holy Spirit at Pentecost. This calling and the empowerment to accomplish it led to experiences that a young fisherman could have never imagined, even in his wildest dreams. When Peter left his nets behind to follow some random Rabbi, he had no idea it would result in him playing a leading role in this resurrection movement that would change the world. But Peter is the personification of the phrase, *It's never too late to be what you might become.* Amid all the mountains and valleys of Peter's story, God continually found space to create something new in this fragile leader.

Now we come to the chapter in Peter's narrative where Jesus' call upon his life—to fish for people—is exponentially multiplied in what has been audaciously called "Absolutely the Most Important Chapter in the Entire Bible."

The Tables Turn

Old Testament scholar Peter Enns writes,

> There is one chapter, in the New Testament, that I think is majorly huge— without it, Christianity as we know does not exist.
>
> And here's the chapter. Ready?
>
> Acts 10.
>
> Bet you didn't see that coming. Bet you thought I was going to pick something about Jesus' birth, crucifixion, or resurrection. But I didn't, did I?
>
> Without Acts 10, you don't go to church on Sunday, have summer youth missions trips, hymnals, cathedrals, Vacation Bible School, or

Contemporary Christian Music. Heck, since so much of western culture reflects nearly 2000 years of Christian influence (and dominance, for ill and good), you could say that without Acts 10, the west as we know it doesn't exist.[9]

Before Acts 10, the lunchroom for followers of Jesus had a distinct and recognizable seating chart. From Acts 10 on, that all changed as the disciples continued to say "Yes, and" to Jesus' vision for the lunchroom.

By the time we arrive in Acts 10, in the decade or so since Pentecost in Acts 2, this movement that is changing the world has grown at breakneck speed. Thousands have come to believe in Jesus, some even outside the home base of Jerusalem. The commission of Acts 1:8—the call to followers to give witness to the liberation found in Jesus *here* (Jerusalem), *there* (Judea and Samaria), *and everywhere* (ends of the earth)—is coming to fruition. And in this "most important chapter in the entire Bible," this call is taken to an unthinkable level as Peter prays on a rooftop in Joppa. He grows hungry, and while lunch is being prepared, he has *"a vision that link[s] his present hunger with what was about to happen"* (Acts 10:10 VOICE, emphasis original). Luke then explains the vision: "[Peter] saw the heaven opened and something like a large sheet coming down, being lowered to the ground by its four corners. In it were all kinds of four-footed creatures and reptiles and birds of the air. Then he heard a voice saying, 'Get up, Peter; kill and eat'" (Acts 10:11–13).

At this moment, the trajectory of Peter's arc hangs in the balance. How will he respond? How slow or fast will he comprehend the magnitude of this vision? He replies to the command to eat by saying, "By no means, Lord, for I have never eaten anything that is profane or unclean" (Acts 10:14). Again, he hears a voice saying, "What God has made clean, you must not call profane" (Acts 10:15). The same thing happens three times, and then the sheet is suddenly taken up to heaven (Acts 10:16). (By the way, two peripheral notes: Have you ever noticed that Peter seems to use the word "no" and "Lord" together far too often in the same sentence? Also, thrice-repeated statements seem to be a theme of Peter's life. At some point, you'd think Peter would say to God, "Yeah, this number three thing ... it's not funny anymore.")

We need to appreciate that obeying the instruction to eat would require Peter to violate the dietary laws clearly laid out in the Torah, which included details about what God's covenantal people could and could not eat. We'll spare you an excursus on the dietary laws of Leviticus 11 and Deuteronomy 14, but it's important to understand that the command given in the vision to Peter contradicted the laws he'd known and sought to follow all his life. In addition to being a part of God's instructions, the dietary laws were one fundamental way that Jews of the time kept their identity as God's people distinct from the Gentiles around them—not because they were "better" than Gentiles but because God had commanded them to be set apart.[10] It was integral to their vocation as a light to the nations. In a time when some of the Hellenistic rulers were trying to erase Jewish identity, the dietary restrictions—and thus who they would share tables with—served to make clear those who were part of God's people and those who weren't. Thus, although a cursory reading of Acts 10 might suggest Peter is being *unfaithful* to God by questioning his command, a deeper reading reveals that Peter is actually trying to be *faithful* to God by rejecting the call to eat. Peter has both some unlearning and relearning to do.

As Peter sorts through his confusion and tries to make sense of this strange vision, three men sent from a God-fearing Gentile named Cornelius arrive. They explain to the confused Peter how Cornelius, a man Peter likely wouldn't share a table with, had experienced his own vision, which involved Peter coming immediately to speak a message at his home in Caesarea. It's possible that at this point, Peter begins to realize this whole episode might be about more than his diet.

The Puzzle Comes Together

In his book detailing the story arc of Peter's life, Michael Card writes, "There comes a moment in our lives when some of the pieces come together—where all our past experiences, both good and bad, are brought to bear in causing us to become who God intends us to be."[11] In many ways, Acts 10 is that moment for Peter, when the puzzle pieces snap into place. It is a defining moment, not only for him but also for this entire movement of Jesus that will make the world a different place.

Peter goes with the men to Cornelius's home, where many are gathered in the hope that Peter will show up. After initial greetings, he stands and begins to speak: "You yourselves know that it is improper for a Jew to associate with or to visit an outsider, but God has shown me that I should not call anyone profane or unclean. So when I was sent for, I came without objection. Now may I ask why you sent for me?" (Acts 10:28–29). Cornelius explains his own vision to Peter and then says, "So now all of us are here in the presence of God to listen to all that the Lord has commanded you to say" (Acts 10:33).

It's possible that Peter understood the significance of these next few moments in this most important chapter in the entire Bible. If he did, this next scene would have been overwhelmingly intense and emotional. Peter was about to stand and speak a word of God's favor and inclusion over a group of people whom he may have previously refused to share a table with to honor his religious convictions. He was about to confess his conviction that God's work in Jesus through the Holy Spirit meant that he could no longer read Scripture in the same way. Peter was about to display his ability to unlearn and relearn. He was being called to see others, Scripture, and God's work in the world differently. For all of Peter's faults, we have to give him credit for being willing to see the lunchroom differently. Few people willingly allow their worldview to be turned on its head this abruptly. (Most go kicking and screaming.)

After a slight pause and deep breath, perhaps with a quiver in his voice, we imagine Peter standing before the crowd and regarding them for the first time as brothers and sisters. He proclaims, "I truly understand that God shows no partiality, but in every people anyone who fears him and practices righteousness is acceptable to him" (Acts 10:34–35, emphasis added).

Don't miss the critical and decisive nature of the phrase "shows no partiality." Also interpreted as "God does not show favoritism" (NIV, NLT) and "God plays no favorites" (MSG, VOICE, TLB), New Testament scholar Darrell Bock explains the phrase this way:

> This term has been found only in Christian works and appears only here in the NT.... The roots of this term go back to the LXX [an abbreviation for

the Septuagint, the name given to the translation of the Old Testament, originally written in Hebrew, into Greek] and Judaism. The word conveys the idea that God "receives faces" or "lifts up the face" that bows to him in acceptance. All have the same potential access to God.[12]

What a beautiful image that is—God lifting up someone's face as a sign of acceptance. Peter's statement as he stands before Cornelius's household is unequivocal: "God shows no partiality." Considering the Old Testament background of this word relating to "receiving faces" or "lifting up the face," Peter is clearly communicating to this Gentile crowd that Jesus has brought to fulfillment a truly powerful and world-changing good news that includes everyone. And if they didn't get that in verse 34 ("God shows no partiality"), they surely would have gotten it in verse 36 ("He is Lord of *all*," emphasis added) and again in verse 43 ("*everyone* who believes in him receives forgiveness of sins through his name," emphasis added). Whether realizing the impact of these words or not, Peter is speaking a powerful message that is good news to all parts of the lunchroom: "Everyone is invited to the table."

A Worldview Reframed

The combination of Peter's vision and Cornelius's testimony about a similar experience was beginning to reframe Peter's worldview—his eating habits, his way of reading Scripture, his social norms, his faith traditions, and those he should or shouldn't share tables with. He now sees the world differently, and so his trajectory is taking quite an unexpected turn.

Peter goes on in Acts 10 to explain the liberating story of Jesus to those who were gathered at Cornelius's home. He provides a highlight reel of Jesus' life and ministry, culminating in verse 43: "All the prophets testify about him that everyone who believes in him receives forgiveness of sins through his name." Apparently, Peter wasn't even close to finishing his talk at this point, as we read that the Holy Spirit suddenly interrupted him and came upon all those listening. "The circumcised believers who had come with Peter were astounded that the gift of the Holy Spirit had been poured out even on the gentiles, for they heard them speaking in tongues and extolling God" (vv. 45–46). They were astounded—amazed, astonished, staggered! Yes, Jesus' forgiveness and God's gift of his Spirit are even for those sitting at all the other tables.

Peter, unable to deny God's work, follows the Spirit's lead to welcome these Gentiles by inviting them in, saying, "Can anyone withhold the water for baptizing these people who have received the Holy Spirit just as we have?" (v. 47). Having clearly seen the connection between baptism and the Holy Spirit for the Jews at Pentecost back in Acts 2, Peter has the Gentiles baptized "in the name of Jesus Christ" (v. 48)—a parallel so strong that many scholars refer to Acts 10 as the "Gentile Pentecost." We can't miss the connection with Galatians 3:27–28, a passage most scholars believe is an early baptism proclamation. There Paul proclaims, "As many of you as were baptized into Christ have clothed yourselves with Christ. There is no longer Jew or Greek; there is no longer slave or free; there is no longer male and female, for all of you are one in Christ Jesus." In baptism, followers of Jesus are taking his name, resulting in distinctions of ethnicity, class, and sex losing their ultimate meaning. All are subsumed under the identity of Jesus. The characteristics so often used to sort people into their various lunch tables lose their priority to the most important thing—the name of Jesus.

What happened that day in Caesarea changed the face of Christianity forever. This narrative is not just about the geographical expansion of the good news of Jesus; it is also a crucial step toward Jesus' prayer in John 17 coming to fruition. This ecclesiology (how they will now gather and structure themselves at one table) that has grown out of their Christology (a foundational belief in Jesus) has given this community of believers completely new horizons for their missiology (a call to go here, there, and everywhere).

In some ways, Gentile inclusion should not have surprised Peter. As God's promise to Abraham reveals all the way back in Genesis, the purpose of Israel's chosenness, of Abraham's descendants being set apart, was so that "in [Abraham] all the families of the earth shall be blessed" (Gen. 12:1–3). The difference in Acts 10, according to New Testament scholar

Matthew Skinner, is that until now these words had "not captured anyone's imagination."[13]

The good news spoken and enacted in Acts 10 is a bold proclamation that bridges the gap between Jews and Gentiles, between insiders and outsiders, between this table and that table. But not everyone is quick to embrace new learning, especially when it's rooted in someone else's experience rather than their own. Back in Jerusalem, the Jewish followers of Jesus initially criticized Peter for eating with Gentiles (Acts 11:2). However, to their credit, when Peter told them the whole story, they joined him on the journey of unlearning and relearning. They responded by praising the undeniable work of God and said, "Then God has given even to the gentiles the repentance that leads to life" (Acts 11:18). This transformative gift given by God sends the community of Jesus-followers on a journey beyond the kind of religious and cultural barriers that all people, then and now, have constructed for themselves. And, in direct application to our ever-so-broken lunchroom, it sends us on a journey to push the tables together.

A Never, Never List

In the late 1800s, Alexander Whyte, minister at St. George's Church in Edinburgh, Scotland, gave a message on Acts 10 and the paradigm-shifting truths contained therein. He described Peter's vision of a large sheet lowered from heaven and carefully recited the list of unclean animals displayed upon it—creatures Peter was instructed to partake of. After recounting Peter's initial resistance to the command to eat, Reverend Whyte concluded his sermon with a practical challenge for the St. George's community:

> If you would, take a four-cornered napkin when you go home, and a pen and ink, and write the names of nations, of politicians, of churches, of neighbors, and fellow-worshippers—all the people you dislike, and despise, and do not, and cannot, and will not, love.
>
> Heap up their names into your unclean napkin, and then look up and say, "Not so, Lord. No way, Lord. Never, Lord. I neither can speak well, nor think well, nor hope well, of these people. I cannot do it, and I will not

try." If you acted out and spoke out all the evil things that are in your heart in some such way as that, you would thus get such a sight of yourselves that you would never forget it.[14]

As each of us ponder our own trajectory toward change, whether slow or fast, as we consider the narrative of Acts 10 and the words God gave Peter to speak in Caesarea, we must ask ourselves: *Who's on my list? Who is on my "never, never list"? Who are the people that I could never imagine sharing a table with? Who are the people I* would *sit with but be resentful toward the whole time? Who are those I wouldn't even consider inviting to any table of mine?* (Seriously, we should all stop for a moment and make our own list.) Perhaps it is time we reconsider our "never, never list" as a list of potential dinner guests. The practice of simply inviting that *someone* to dinner powerfully counteracts a culture where our dinner lists only include people who are like us.

Maybe the dinner is literal—actually inviting someone over—or maybe it involves another first step. Perhaps "inviting someone to dinner" looks like reading a book by an author with different theological convictions, taking a posture that genuinely seeks to understand their perspective. Maybe "inviting someone to dinner" looks like finding a way to partner with a church whose sordid history with our own should probably be water under the bridge. Or it could be that "inviting someone to dinner" looks like reaching out to someone on our "never, never list" (or maybe even on our "meh, no thanks list") and trying to find those convictions and beliefs about Jesus that we *do* have in common.

If our invitation lists for dinner are to expand, if we are to *be what we might become,* there is much that must change. Reflecting on the experience Peter had at Cornelius's home, Skinner writes,

> Attitudes will have to adjust. Practices will have to expand or change. Strangers will have to be greeted. Customs will evolve. God's intrusive activity involves much more than helping Peter figure out what he's permitted to eat for his midafternoon snack. As a result of this particular disruption, the church will never be the same again.[15]

We have a decision similar to Peter's to make: Will our response to Jesus' vision for the lunchroom be "By no means!" or "Yes, and"? Will we refuse to unlearn and relearn, or will we allow the trajectories of our stories to be changed, however messy that may be? Do we really believe that, whether slow or fast, it's never too late to be what we might become?

Searching for a
Theological Imagination

You can love without agreeing with someone.
You can disagree without hating them.
TIMOTHY KELLER

It is exactly in common searches and shared tasks
that new ideas are born, that new visions reveal
themselves and that new roads become visible.
HENRI NOUWEN

"You're gonna need a bigger boat."—Martin Brody, *Jaws*
"You can't handle the truth!"—Colonel Jessup, *A Few Good Men*
"Here's looking at you, kid."—Rick Blaine, *Casablanca*
"I'm the king of the world!"—Jack Dawson, *Titanic*[1]

Each of these quotes is a strong contender for the all-time most famous movie line. The irony, though, is that not a single one was in the original script for the movie or discussed with the director before the actors delivered them. Each line was completely improvised. Yet, far from being haphazard additions, these famous lines built on the established narrative, were rooted in the script, and were perfectly consistent with the character's voice. Ultimately, each of those lines added something new while remaining faithful to the story—lines it's hard to imagine weren't there originally.

As we continue to examine how the early church began to push the tables of their broken lunchroom together, consider the following "improvised" line: "Therefore I have reached the decision that we should not trouble those gentiles who are turning to God" (Acts 15:19). Although it may not have quite the same ring as "Leave the gun, take the cannoli" (an unscripted line in the 1972 classic *The Godfather*),[2] this line, when spoken in the context of Acts 15, carried surprising weight. Its influence dramatically shaped the story of God the early church lived out in ACT V of our biblical narrative.

Reading Acts through the lens of faithful improvisation can spark our own imaginations for transforming the lunchroom in ways that better align with Jesus' vision. Eric Barreto reminds us that the narratives in Acts aren't just stories to imitate, nor are they merely historical remembrances of better days long gone: "Instead, the theology of Luke-Acts is primarily *imaginative*, precisely because it is set within a narrative framework. We are searching for a theological imagination that can encourage prophetic action, compassionate care, and a communal identity open to God's transformative activity among and with us."[3] A "theological imagination" is a crucial component of faithful improvisation.

New Testament scholar Luke Timothy Johnson refines this way of reading Acts even further:

> The first readers of Luke's narrative would perhaps not have seen his story as a nostalgic recollection of a time past but rather as a summons to an ideal that might be in danger of being lost, not as a work of bland historiography but as a thrilling act of utopian imagination, less a neutral report on how things were than as a normative prescription for how things ought to be.[4]

The "ideal" Johnson talks about—the "utopian imagination" and "how things ought to be"—is calling us forward to ACT VI, where the transformation of our world is finally complete. *That* is the improvisational story we are attempting to join and the impetus behind our call to "Yes, and."

Those who excel at improvisation realize that this art is not merely imitative, not simply impersonating one famous actor after another. The *best* improv is primarily imaginative precisely because it is set within a narrative framework. It explores new frontiers within that framework and creates a new path forward while staying true to the story thus far. The *worst* of improv defaults to stereotypes, mimicking what has already been done rather than constructing what could be.[5] If we understand Scripture as one story from beginning to end of God putting his family back together—an understanding that prompts us to discern our role in the restoration of all things—we believe we are both called and commissioned to "thrilling acts of utopian imagination" and "faithful improvisation." Rather than merely dictating our behaviors, the book of Acts shapes how we imagine our place in this grand narrative and how we understand our relation to others within the story. If we let it, this reshaped imagination can help us see people at other tables "as partners in faithful discernment, not as foreign threats or strange folks one must merely tolerate."[6]

In Acts, we see followers of Jesus regularly positioned at unexpected tables with surprising table fellows. Yet in all the surprising diversity and difference, they find ways to faithfully improvise and inch closer to pushing together the tables of a fractured world.

A Critical Question

We've told the stories of Philip and Peter as examples of the early Jesus-followers attempting to live in a way that was faithful to the story before them while also discerning what the new work of God through Jesus meant for Samaritans, eunuchs, and Gentiles. We left off the last chapter in Acts 10, with Peter unequivocally proclaiming that God shows no partiality—that the gospel is for *all*, even the Gentiles.

Although that particular scene may have ended, the faithful improvisation was just beginning. The early Christians still had to figure out what a "gospel for *all*" would actually look like. They had to discern what, if any, conditions were required for Gentiles (i.e., non-Jews) to be included among God's people. Earlier in ACT III (before Jesus' life, death, and resurrection), God had said that circumcision was the everlasting sign of his covenant with Abraham and his descendants (Israel). Genesis 17 is quite explicit that *every* male offspring of Abraham should be circumcised. Failure to do so meant a breaking of God's covenant and resulted in the individual being cut off from God's people (Gen. 17:14). In ACT IV (during Jesus' time), God's people—including Jesus—continued to be circumcised as a sign of their covenant relationship with God (Luke 2:21). Historical documents from that period confirm not only that Jews continued to circumcise their sons but also that any man who fully converted to Judaism would also undergo circumcision.[7] Circumcision, along with Sabbath observance and following the Levitical dietary regulations, were three of the key ways that God's people (Israel) were set apart from the nations (Gentiles).

So at the beginning of ACT V (the expansion of the church), the critical question became: Did all those who proclaimed that the God of Israel had become incarnate as a Jewish man have to obey the covenant instructions for Israel (i.e., the Torah), even though they weren't Jewish? Again, Acts 10–14 confirmed that Gentiles could be a part of the covenant people (and arguably the Great Commission in Matthew 28:18–20 and the Ascension Commission in Acts 1:8 *necessitate* their inclusion). However, the early Christians hadn't yet worked out the logistics of what that looked like, particularly concerning the key identity markers of God's people—circumcision, dietary laws, and Sabbath observance. Would those who weren't Jews have to observe Jewish dietary laws or honor the Sabbath? Would they have to undergo circumcision? In other words, did pushing the lunchroom tables together mean that Gentiles would have to become like Jews?

Could these two groups with such different lived experiences—including when they worked, what they ate, and what holidays they observed—really be united as one people? Was there any hope that "they may all be one ... so that the world may believe that [the Father] sent [the Son]" (John 17:21)?

Cue Acts 15.

Things Are about to Get Messy

In Acts 15, after Peter's experience in Caesarea, news spread quickly that something significant had occurred at the home of Cornelius, a Gentile.

The significance of this event—the Gentile Pentecost—was becoming increasingly apparent. The word on the street was that life in the lunchroom had changed forever. But such a profound paradigm shift inevitably sparked intense and fierce disagreements: Who was allowed to participate in this movement, and what requirements must be met for membership?

Paul and Barnabas (more on them in a minute) had "no small dissension and debate" with some fellow Jewish believers from Judea (Acts 15:2) over this question of Gentile inclusion. As convenient as it would have been, God did not send a dove from heaven with a scroll entitled, "Here's what to do with those Gentiles!" That is, he didn't just give them a script to memorize and act out. He trusted them to improvise faithfully as they sought to understand what was happening to the lunchroom they thought they knew so well. And they *didn't* respond like many church leaders do today:

- They didn't brush it under the rug. ("What if people realize we don't have it all figured out? What if they think we're not united?")
- They didn't appeal thoughtlessly to tradition. ("But we've always done it this way.")
- They didn't just have the one with the most power, authority, or charisma make a unilateral decision. ("Those at the top know what's best!")
- They didn't let the debate turn into division ("We can't agree, so we're going to start our own thing over there.")

No, at the Jerusalem Council,[8] God's people, as a diverse community, accompanied by the promised Holy Spirit (Acts 15:28), wrestled through Scripture, their religious traditions, and their experiences of God. Together, they thoughtfully discerned what living faithfully looked like in their time and place as the lunchroom was starting to look remarkably different.[9] Although it would have been easier to avoid the hard conversations and form separate tables based on theological preference, the early church had the courage to choose the more challenging path. Despite their disagreements, they committed to making sure the tables stayed pushed together.

It was messy. Improvisation almost always is.

But it was also beautiful. Improvisation *sometimes* is.

The characters on the stage in Acts 15 stepped into an unknown reality, relying on both the story thus far and a willingness to listen attentively to one another. Several different parties contributed to the Jerusalem Council. First were some believers who were Pharisees.[10] Second were Paul and Barnabas, two of the leading missionaries of the early church. Last were "the apostles and the elders," which included James (the brother of Jesus and leader of the Jerusalem church) and Peter.

Luke tells us that, like the initial "dissension and debate" that prompted the Council (Acts 15:2), the meeting itself was also characterized by "much debate" (Acts 15:7). (Think of the Thanksgiving table when the subject of banning certain books enters the conversation before anyone's had a bite of turkey. We're talking *that* kind of "much debate.") We want to explore the rest of the Jerusalem Council story and the characters involved to help us think about the messy-yet-beautiful process of faithful improvisation in our lunchroom today.

"Well, the Scriptures Say"

First, we have the Christian Pharisees (Acts 15:5). The Christian Pharisees unequivocally refer to Scripture—which at that time was what we call the Old Testament—to make their case: "It is necessary for them [i.e., Gentiles] to be circumcised and ordered to keep the law of Moses" (Acts 15:5). Though Luke doesn't give us a book, chapter, and verse for their argument (not that he could, since there were no chapter or verse divisions in the first century), their advocacy for circumcision is no doubt referring to Genesis 17, discussed earlier, where God clearly outlined the stipulations of his covenant with Abraham: "This is my covenant, which you shall keep, between me and you and your offspring after you: Every male among you shall be circumcised. ... it shall be a sign of the covenant between me and you" (Gen. 17:10–11). Multiple times in the wider passage, God emphasized that this covenant should be kept throughout the generations (Gen. 17:9, 12). It was part of an "everlasting" covenant (Gen. 17:13, 19).

We imagine the Christian Pharisees at the Jerusalem Council asking the others, "What part of *everlasting* don't you understand!" Their interpretation of Scripture, including Genesis 17 and the Torah as a whole, gave them a clear and obvious answer to the issue—Gentiles could only become part of God's people by undergoing circumcision and following the laws of the Torah. Who was going to argue with that! For them, ACT III was a script they were to memorize and follow rather than a larger story from which they were to faithfully improvise. They embraced the "Yes" but not the "and."

"But Did You See What God Did!"

Second, we have Peter (Acts 15:7–11), followed by Paul and Barnabas (Acts 15:12). Peter makes the opposite argument—Gentiles will be saved by grace, not circumcision or full Torah observance. He justifies his argument with an appeal to his experience of God's work at that time, as they were trying to live out ACT V.[11] Pointing to the story narrated in Acts 10–11 with Cornelius, Peter explains, "God, who knows the human heart, testified to them [i.e., the Gentiles] by giving them the Holy Spirit, *just as he did to us*, and in cleansing their hearts by faith he has made no distinction between them and us" (Acts 15:8–9, emphasis added). When Peter witnessed the Gentiles receiving God's Spirit just as Peter's own people had, he couldn't deny that God was at work.[12]

But this wasn't just an individual, subjective experience. Cornelius's experience—a vision from an angel—helped Peter interpret his own vision. Johnson points out that Peter didn't understand the full meaning of "what God has made clean" in Acts 10:15, so he asked Cornelius—a person "with the religious experience of someone outside the historical people of God"—to help him understand it.[13] Additionally, other believers from Joppa accompanied Peter to Cornelius's house (Acts 10:23) and witnessed the events that unfolded there. They were the ones who were astonished that God was pouring out his Spirit even on the Gentiles (Acts 10:45). Eventually, even the Christian community in Jerusalem affirmed Peter's experience of Gentile inclusion (Acts 11:18). Johnson explains that validation from other believers, both from Joppa and Jerusalem, "raises Peter's act from the private to the communal level."[14]

Furthermore, at the end of his speech, Peter wrestles with the weight of his religious tradition. He asks, "Why are you putting God to the test by placing on the neck of the disciples a yoke that neither our ancestors nor we have been able to bear?" (Acts 15:10). Although other portions of Scripture speak about the law very differently (e.g., Psalm 119), Peter here suggests that the Christian Pharisees' proposal goes beyond Scripture's good intention and could potentially overburden Gentile Christians.[15] In essence, Peter is trying to say that they were demanding the Gentile believers do something that they themselves could not.

The argument of Paul and Barnabas (Acts 15:12) is similar to Peter's—an appeal to their experience of God's work, specifically those narrated earlier in Acts: "They told of all the signs and wonders that God had done through them among the gentiles" (Acts 15:12). A close reader of Acts knows that the phrase "signs and wonders" is Luke's way of describing how God validates human ministry.[16] In this case, they are pointing to what had happened on their previous missionary journey (Acts 13–14), where, because of repeated rejection from Jews, Paul and Barnabas announced, "We are now turning to the gentiles. For so the Lord has commanded us, saying, 'I have set you to be a light for the gentiles, so that you may bring salvation to the ends of the earth'" (Acts 13:46–47, quoting Isa. 49:6).

Paul and Barnabas shared this experience (i.e., "all that God had done with them, and how he had opened a door of faith for the gentiles") with the church in Antioch, which had commended their work (Acts 14:26–27). Just as Peter's experience was affirmed and elevated to a communal level through the presence of other believers, so, too, were Paul and Barnabas's encounters of God's work among the Gentiles validated by the church. Paul and Barnabas don't say much—their first-hand experience of God's activity among the Gentiles suffices as their argument. Like Peter, they were fully committed to the improvisation needed in ACT V.

"Hear Me Out . . . What if There Was Just One Table?"

Lastly, we come to James (Acts 15:13–21), the leader of the Council, whose role in the narrative is critical. First and foremost, he prioritizes bringing each group to the table, ensuring every perspective is represented. Then he ensures they stay at the table long enough to hear and be heard by others. He reasons through each of the viewpoints as well as through other Scriptures to navigate a way forward for the early church.

James accepts Peter's experience of God among the Gentiles and notes how it agrees with Scripture, though a different Scripture than that appealed to by the Pharisees. He takes the experience of God working among the Gentiles via Peter and says that the words of the prophet agree with it (interestingly, *not* that Peter's experience agrees with the prophets).[17] He quotes Amos 9:11–12, where the prophet foretells a time when Gentiles would seek the Lord. Surprisingly, this passage doesn't address the practical application that the Jerusalem Council sought—they'd already agreed that Gentiles were allowed a seat at the table. The question they were trying to answer was *what stipulations* (circumcision, etc.) the Gentiles had to adhere to for inclusion in the movement. The Christian Pharisees' Scripture actually addressed this logistical question ("Yes! Gentiles must be circumcised and keep all of the Torah!"), but James's Scripture didn't; it merely confirmed that the restored people of God included both Jew and Gentile. The Christian Pharisees argue that they had the script—if the others would just learn and execute the clear-cut lines (pun intended), they could move on to saving the world!

But James doesn't view earlier parts of Scripture as providing a script for his present time. His conclusion does not accept the Christian Pharisees' Scripture as giving a clear and obvious solution to their dilemma. Instead, he concludes that Gentiles do *not* have to be circumcised and observe all of the Torah to have a seat at the table. ACT v is not the same as ACTS iii and iv. James, like Peter, wrestles with some of his religious traditions ("Yes"), wondering how they might inform what faithful improvisation ("and") looks like.

James explains, "For in every city, for generations past, Moses has had those who proclaim him, for he has been read aloud every Sabbath in the synagogues" (Acts 15:21). In other words, because Jewish Christians continued to observe Jewish practices, as they had across both time ("for generations past") and space ("in every city"), Gentiles should submit to a small number of less burdensome practices for the sake of fellowship with the body. (Surely we can all see how asking someone to avoid meat sacrificed to idols is one thing, while asking adult male converts to be circumcised is quite another!)

James doesn't forbid Gentiles from eating meat with blood because Leviticus 17:10 forbids it but because doing so would enable Jewish Christians (who didn't cease being Jews or practicing the Torah when they became Christians) and Gentile Christians to share a table. James knew that commensality was a core part of the vision Jesus had cast in ACT IV that they needed to embody. How could Jesus' disciples claim to be one with one another (John 17) if they couldn't even eat together? An inability to come around a table together would not be saying "Yes" to Luke 14 or John 17.

Careful Listening

Why are we spending so much time exploring how those at the beginning of ACT V used improvisation to try to faithfully continue the story that spanned ACTS I through IV? If we're not merely to repeat the lines and imitate Peter, Paul, or James, what's the point? As we discussed in chapter six, successful improv involves careful listening, not just to the script from earlier ACTS, but also to the characters in our own ACT—not just the characters at our own tables, though, but from all different parts of the lunchroom. And as distant as the mid-first-century Jerusalem Council is from today, it is nonetheless the beginning of ACT V, the ACT we are still faithfully improvising today.

If we listen carefully, there is much to learn, not just about *what* the early Christians decided but about *how* they improvised well. Faithful improvisation is a *dynamic* task—it's not fixed, it doesn't have a rulebook to follow, and it's not always predictable. As we said earlier, faithful improvisation is messy and rarely linear. At the Jerusalem Council, there were multiple characters and perspectives, each appealing to different sources of authority, sometimes in seemingly opposing ways. It involved "much debate" (Acts 15:7), with different Scriptures and solutions proposed and honest wrestling with religious traditions. Yet they didn't let their disagreements or the lack of a tidy process divide them. We should expect our current attempts at living faithfully to be similarly messy (and hopefully also similarly beautiful).

How can we reconcile the fact that both sides of the debate appeal to Scripture to support opposing viewpoints? This shouldn't be new to us. Pro-slavery advocates pointed to Scripture, and anti-slavery advocates did, too. Complementarians point to Scripture, and so do egalitarians. Unfortunately, Scripture can be made to say almost anything when viewed as isolated sound bites. Remember, even Satan pointed to Scripture in the temptation narratives! This is why we need a more thoughtful view of Scripture that goes beyond just pointing to random passages here and there.

We believe reading Scripture in light of the larger narrative, with an attempt to move the story *forward* to new creation, not *backward* to an earlier ACT, helps us avoid such pitfalls. Suffice it to say, we believe that the Jerusalem Council shows us that faithful improvisation must entail more than simply pointing to Scriptures that confirm what we already believe. It must include listening to the breadth of Scripture, being willing to put our traditions on the table (both the good and the bad), and remaining open to the ways God is at work in the world. Our current lunchroom will not align with Jesus' vision if we keep doing what we've always done. We must say "Yes," and we must also say "and."

The Four "Cs"

If you've ever had the opportunity to see improv live or watch a production as ingenious as *Middleditch and Schwartz* (a completely improvised one-hour, two-person show on Netflix), then you've witnessed the power of improvisation. With only a minuscule part of a narrative already assembled, these artists invite the audience into a story that almost feels like magic, an adventure far beyond what they could have imagined at the start. The early followers of

Jesus were invited into this far-beyond adventure in the book of Acts, and we are invited into it as well. We have a responsibility to continue ACT V faithfully.

The director of ImprovBoston's National Touring Company, Deana Criess, teaches what she calls "The Four Cs of Improv": "collaboration, creativity, critical thinking, and communication."[18] We believe that the Jerusalem Council embodied these four Cs and invited the larger community of Jesus-followers into a way of being the church that stretched their imaginations beyond the lunchroom status quo.

Consider those four Cs in the faithful improvisation led by James in Acts 15.

Collaboration: The captivating sequence of events at the Jerusalem Council first reminds us that theology is best done communally rather than individually. Yes, James, the leader of the Jerusalem Church, "reach[es] the decision" (Acts 15:19), but he does so in consideration with the apostles and elders (Acts 15:6) and by deliberately making space for different people with different perspectives to come together. We imagine James hearing the Christian Pharisees' perspective and quickly responding with a "Yes, and," then enthusiastically pointing to Peter to speak. When Peter concludes, it is, "Yes, and." James finally points to Paul and Barnabas, who then bring in their perspective. It's a collective endeavor, not a solo one.

Creativity: This collaboration is what fueled the creativity of the Council. Recognizing the way forward was yet to be created, James realized something powerful was happening in the room amid the community's many voices. In light of the undeniable works of God, they could not merely keep repeating lines from earlier ACTS of the play. They had to creatively discern what was right at *this* moment in *this* ACT. The new faithful way of living came to fruition through the creativity (and we would add courage) of those willing to recognize that moment in time called for something different.

Critical Thinking: After carefully listening to others' experiences, James and the others were forced to ask questions they hadn't considered before to assess and address what was most important in this discussion. This involved weighing multiple Scriptures, encounters with God, and views of how God was working in the world. Ultimately, with an empathetic assessment that took into account multiple different hermeneutics and religious experiences, along with a commitment not to unduly create barriers for those genuinely wanting to follow Jesus, they reached a conclusion. This was not an example of "The Bible says it, I believe it, that settles it" masquerading as theology. It was deep, it was hard, and it required much debate and thought.

Communication: Eventually, the apostles, elders, and "the whole church" (Acts 15:22) agreed on how to implement this monumental decision. Not only did they write a letter to send to the Gentile believers to inform them of their decision, but they also sent the letter with Judas and Silas to tell them themselves. (We can almost hear the sigh of relief followed by a loud cheer when the men found out they didn't, in fact, have to be circumcised.)

These four Cs were a crucial part of how the early church improvised well and are undoubtedly informative for our own attempts at faithful improvisation.

Jesus cast the vision for a new kind of lunchroom—one that seeks to heal the brokenness of Genesis 3, that refuses to let The Three Ds of Disconnection have the last word, that takes seriously the pronouncement that "there is still room" at the Master's table, and that is fiercely committed to oneness with God and each another. Though the mission was never easy and rarely without problems, these wet-behind-the-ears disciples in Luke's account of "thirty years that changed the world" nonetheless attempted to faithfully embody Jesus' vision for the lunchroom in their time and place. They said "Yes" to Jesus' example of sitting at the table with those they didn't always see eye to eye with, and they embraced the "and" of being open to those whom God was calling them to invite to the table. We want to do the same thing. In the remaining chapters, we'll offer three ways we might do that—in the way we view others, in the conversations we have, and in the ways we gather.

The Divine Spark

The problem is, many of the people in need of saving are in churches, and at least part of what they need saving from is the idea that God sees the world the same way they do.
BARBARA BROWN TAYLOR

The supreme religious challenge is to see God's image in one who is not in our image.
RABBI JONATHAN SACKS

Before entering into this next chapter, wait for just a minute. Breathe deeply. Pause and reflect on the story we have attempted to tell in the previous chapters.

In chapter one, we described a social and spiritual setting in our world that too closely resembles a dysfunctional high school lunchroom. In chapters two and three, we explored the sociological and theological roots of our brokenness. This brokenness is not God's good intent, as seen in Genesis 1–2, but permeates the scriptural narrative from Genesis 3 to today. As we urged in chapters four and five, there is hope for a way forward if we consider a deep and consummate change of paradigm and aspire to a bigger table—one that more closely resembles both the practices of Jesus and the fruition of his prayer for two kinds of oneness in John 17. In chapters six through nine, we entered the stories of the earliest followers of Jesus in

Acts as they unlearned and relearned a different way to live within the first-century lunchroom in the wake of Jesus' resurrection.

Thus far we've focused primarily on the *narrative* texts in the Bible, especially Genesis, the Gospels, and Acts. Faithful improvisation has been a crucial metaphor as we've tried to find our own role in these narratives of Scripture. And yet after Acts, the rest of the New Testament books aren't narratives. Instead, they're primarily letters, with a sermon (Hebrews) and apocalypse (Revelation) sprinkled in. We believe the New Testament letters are nonetheless deeply rooted in the larger narrative of God's redemptive work in the world. Many of the letters follow a similar structure—painting a picture of the story of God thus far, establishing the significance of Jesus' work, and calling the original listeners to live their lives in light of that story.

These calls to live differently are often marked by a crucial word: "therefore." Ephesians and Galatians are great examples of this—in the earlier chapters (Eph. 1–3; Gal. 1–4), Paul invites the readers into the story of the redemptive work of Christ, which, he argues, transforms their identity. He then inserts a clear "therefore" (Eph. 4:1; Gal 5:1), a call to consider how the story of Jesus dramatically impacts how they are to live their lives now, be it in unity with the church (Eph. 4:2–13), how their family life operates (Eph. 5:21–6:9), or how to live life in community (Gal. 5:19–6:5).

Paul uses this same rhetorical move in what is likely his most famous New Testament letter: Romans. Contrary to common belief, Paul's letter to the Christians in Rome is not simply a theological treatise designed to guide its readers to a richer and deeper systematic understanding of the doctrines of God (though, of course, it does do that). Romans is also a beautiful story that reveals God's faithfulness and mercy to *all* people—both Jews and Gentiles—through Jesus.

After telling that story in Romans 1–11, Paul makes the literary shift. Starting in chapter 12, he pleads with the Romans: "I appeal to you *therefore*, brothers and sisters, on the basis of God's mercy, to present your bodies as a living sacrifice, holy and acceptable to God, which is your reasonable act of worship" (Rom. 12:1, emphasis added). "On the basis of God's mercy" is an appeal to the story he'd told in the previous eleven chapters—they must say "yes" to that story. But they must also move that story forward. Paul's "therefore" in Romans 12 is the "and" of faithful improvisation. Paul follows this appeal with eighty-some verses (Rom. 12–15) of what it might look like for the Roman Christians to live faithfully in ACT V. Far from being lines or stage directions for his audience to deliver passively, Paul is urging his fellow believers to actively grapple with what faithful living looks like in their own context. The call is to thought*ful* participation rather than thought*less* recitation.

We all need a good "therefore."

And so, we now want to think more concretely about what faithful and practical living looks like in our own lunchroom contexts. We want to ask how we can resist the lunchroom dynamic that tries to sort us into divided tables and instead learn new and faithful ways to play our roles in this narrative "so that the world may believe" (John 17:21). These final chapters in the book are our "therefore."

A Posture of Generous Spaciousness

As we begin to put the practical "therefore" wheels on this engine, we want to consider our posture—not the straightness of our back but our attitude, outlook, and approach. Cultural commentator Andy Crouch notes, "Our posture is our learned but unconscious default position, our natural stance. It is the position our body assumes when we aren't paying attention, the basic attitude we carry through life."[1] We all have certain postures in the lunchroom, though they may differ depending on who we're with, what we're talking about, or what table we've gathered at. Unfortunately, most of our postures have been impacted by The Three Ds of Disconnection (distance, distortion, and distrust). Our posture might keep people at arm's length, make us defensive, or cause us to be fearful or suspicious. "Often," Crouch notes, "it's difficult to discern our own posture."[2]

Difficult as our posture may be to discern, we not only believe it's possible to do so but also that our posture is malleable. Yes, Roy, people can change. It's never too late to be who we might become, remember?

Our "therefore," we believe, looks like a *generous* posture, though the specifics of what that looks like will vary for each of us. When we talk about being "generous," we're not talking about money or possessions (though Jesus *did* have plenty to say about that). We're talking about being generous in how we see others, how we have conversations, and how we gather. Wendy VanderWal-Gritter, executive director of Generous Space Ministries, describes this posture well with her definition of "generous spaciousness":

> Generous spaciousness humbly acknowledges our limitations and intentionally chooses a posture of listening and learning. It recognizes that among those who identify as followers of Jesus and have a high regard for Scripture, there are diverse perspectives on many different questions … in regard to how to live as a faithful disciple of Christ. Despite these differences, generous spaciousness makes room for us to join in conversation together in a shared quest for a deeper and more robust relationship with Christ…. [It] fearlessly extends room to others to explore and grow in faith. Generous spaciousness is decidedly relational. It isn't a theoretical concept to argue about but an interpersonal reality to be lived. Generous spaciousness sees generosity in God's heart.[3]

Don't miss that last point—that this generous posture is ultimately rooted in God's generosity to us. We prioritize giving freely in relationships and living in the lunchroom in ways that don't expect anything in return. Why? Because God has been generous toward us; he is the generous host who boldly proclaims, "There is still room" (Luke 14:22).

A posture of generosity, of course, must be learned. It must be practiced. It doesn't come naturally, but we believe that with the Spirit—promised as part of the deep change of rebirth—alongside a willingness to unlearn and relearn, we can set right our posture.

The Only Winning Move

War Games is a 1983 movie starring Matthew Broderick as David Lightman, a high school computer genius who hacks into the school computer to change his grades. Stumbling across something called "Global Thermonuclear War," which he assumes to be a game, he unwittingly finds himself logged into a United States military supercomputer. David ends up activating a protocol to start a nuclear war that will surely prompt World War III.

At the end of the film, all attempts to regain control and cancel the countdown to nuclear annihilation have failed. In a last-ditch effort to save the world, David directs the computer to play Tic-tac-toe against itself. As it does, the computer realizes there's no way to win—it only draws—and so it learns the concept of futility.

As the countdown to war approaches, and the huge computer screens flash faster and faster, the computer realizes the results in Global Thermonuclear War are as futile as trying to get three Xs in a row in Tic-tac-toe. Sharing this newfound knowledge on its screen, the computer types out:

Greetings ...
A strange game.
The only winning move is not to play.[4]

We live in a world where sometimes it can feel like we've stumbled into a war zone, a lunchroom where everyone must choose a side, everyone must declare an allegiance, everyone must pick their table. It's a label-making, t-shirt-displaying, badge-wearing[5] world where everyone needs a team and must display their team's color and logo boldly. We want to make sure there's no doubt which side we're on when it comes to this or that theological idea, this or that candidate, this or that person who needs to be condemned, this or that side of whatever issue we're told we must have a statement about. And, of course, our churches also succumb—is your church attractional or missional? Maybe it's an emergent or a seeker church? Is it traditional or progressive? Is it red or blue? And on and on and on.

But who says we have to play the game? Surely by choosing sides, we're only exacerbating the distance, distortion, and distrust. It seems that many of us are weary of playing, but we keep showing up because it appears to be the only option. But if enough of us refuse to engage, wouldn't the game stop? Is it even a competition if only one side plays?

We believe that Jesus' vision for the lunchroom frees us from playing the "us versus them" game. Our "therefore"—our posture of generosity—refuses to play the game that views others as rivals or bullies or kids with their backs against the wall. It refuses to play the game that resorts to shouting matches that prioritize being heard above hearing others. It refuses to play the game that only gathers with those at our own table or requires uniformity to belong. Can we learn what the supercomputer in *War Games* learned—that *the only winning move is not to play?*

We think we can, and it starts with adopting a generous posture. In chapters eleven and twelve, we'll consider how we can be generous in our *conversations* and how we *gather*. But first, in the remainder of this chapter, we want to explore how we can be generous in how we *see each other*, particularly by paying attention to others and seeing them for what they are first and foremost—created in the image of God.

Love = Attention. Attention = Love

The 2017 movie *Lady Bird* focuses on the life of high-school senior Christine McPherson, or "Lady Bird," as she renames herself. Full of angst about her mother and her future in her hometown, it initially appears to be a typical coming-of-age teenage movie. But beneath the exterior of eighteen-year-old fear and anxiety is a strong but subtle theme about the ways we view the world and the people around us. The movie celebrates the beauty of making space to love each other if we learn to pay attention. This is encapsulated in a scene where Lady Bird meets with a nun at her school to discuss her college future and her desire to escape her hometown of Sacramento, California.

Sister Sarah Joan tells Lady Bird, "I read your college essay. You clearly love Sacramento."

"I do?" Lady Bird asks skeptically.

"You write about Sacramento so affectionately and with such care," the nun explains.

"I was just describing it," Lady Bird responds, not seeing the significance.

The nun gently insists, "Well, it comes across as love."

"Sure, I guess I pay attention," Lady Bird replies.

And with simplistic wisdom, Sister Sarah Joan asks a deeper question: "Don't you think maybe they are the same thing? Love and attention?"[6]

The importance of paying attention is a concept explored by many thinkers, including the French philosopher Simone Weil, who wrote that "attention is the rarest and purest form of generosity."[7] Weil suggests that by turning our full attention to someone, listening to them without distraction or prejudice, and truly understanding their ideas and perspectives, we show them that they are worth our time—"the rarest and purest form of generosity."

David Brooks, in his book *How To Know A Person: The Art of Seeing Others Deeply and Being Deeply Seen*, puts it another way: "There is one skill that lies at the heart of any healthy person, family, school, community organization, or society: the ability to see someone else deeply and make them feel seen—to accurately know another person, to let them feel valued, heard, and understood."[8] This ability to generously see each other with this level of attentiveness doesn't come naturally for most. It's not reflexive or instinctual. But a commitment to connecting beyond the surface level helps us move toward a different kind of lunchroom.

Dribbling with Your Head Up

To excel at either basketball or football/soccer—the two most beautiful games[9]—requires the skill of keeping the ball under control while still paying attention to the flow of the entire game. "Dribbling with your head up" is therefore a skill that must be mastered early on. The inability to see others generously is similar to an inability to dribble with your head up. Going through life with our heads down and eyes lowered, lacking awareness of others due to our self-absorption—these postures keep us from seeing each other generously.

To achieve what Weil labeled the "rarest and purest form of generosity" requires us to learn to see the world beyond our normal purview. However, that can be quite a considerable task when we realize how little attention we actually pay to anything that doesn't involve ourselves and our already-established beliefs. The reasons for our narrow, restricted view of those sitting at other tables in the lunchroom vary, but if we're willing to look up, pay attention, and see others differently, the lunchroom starts to look a little more like God intended.

Author David Foster Wallace, in his well-known commencement address at Kenyon College in 2005, implored his audience to pursue a critical awareness about themselves and those who live around them by "altering or getting free of [their] natural, hard-wired default setting which is to be deeply and literally self-centered and to see and interpret everything through this lens of self."[10] He proposed that they learn to live life outside of their own limited perspectives (dribbling with their heads up, if you will) as a starting point for giving generous attention in every situation, especially those where they may have already drawn uncharitable conclusions.

Foster Wallace describes numerous day-to-day, mind-numbing situations that we all experience, where we have the option either to pay attention or to simply default to our self-awarded throne at the center of the world. One example he describes is the individuals we may encounter in the tedious wait in the line at the grocery store at the end of a long workday:

> Most days, if you're aware enough to give yourself a choice, you can choose to look differently at this ... dead-eyed, over-made-up lady who just screamed at her kid in the checkout line. Maybe she's not usually like this. Maybe she's been up three straight nights holding the hand of a husband who is dying of bone cancer. Or maybe this very lady is the low-wage clerk at the motor vehicle department, who just yesterday helped your spouse resolve a horrific, infuriating, red-tape problem through some small act of bureaucratic kindness. Of course, none of this is likely, but it's also not impossible. It just depends what you want to consider. If you're automatically sure that you know what reality is, and you are operating on your default setting, then you, like me, probably won't consider possibilities that aren't annoying and miserable. But if you really learn how to pay attention, then you will know there are other options.

It will actually be within your power to experience a crowded, hot, slow, consumer-hell type situation as not only meaningful, but sacred.[11]

Foster Wallace's point is powerful: We have a choice in how we view others. This act of paying attention to others and adopting a generous posture toward them holds the potential to be a sacred act—and can start transforming the broken lunchroom culture. Maybe it starts with the table next to ours, the one we can at least *tolerate*. Perhaps we can begin to consider the reasons why that church or those believers we know have a different political preference to us. Or why their styles of worship and preaching are different. Or why their beliefs about leadership are different. Perhaps we can be open to them having potentially good reasons for these choices, with positive motivations, even if we disagree with their conclusions. With that realization and an openness to get to know more about those who are different from us, we walk through the lunchroom differently. Instead of continuing to stroll to our same table with our heads down every single day, we choose to see others and start pulling up a chair to their table or inviting them to push their table up to ours. And gradually, through the rarest and purest form of generosity, the lunchroom culture begins to shift.

Before Forward, Back

Thus far we've talked about choices we can make to help us view others generously, such as paying attention to others, trying to see others deeply, and deliberately resisting the urge to focus on ourselves. But we want to make sure we are crystal clear in *why* being generous in how we see others is part of our "therefore." This posture is more than good advice from an Oscar-nominated film or some of the great thinkers of our day. This posture is deeply rooted in God's intent for his creation and was consistently modeled by Jesus. And so we believe the way forward is actually to start by going backward—to remind ourselves of how this grand story of God, the grand story of us all, actually began.

The way forward remembers that the story starts with "then God said, 'Let us make humans in our image, according to our likeness'" (Gen 1:26), and *not* "she took of its fruit and ate, and she also gave some to her husband, who was with her, and he ate" (Gen 3:6). Perceiving that each and every person is made in the image of God leads to an entirely different way of seeing each other.

Missiologist Debra Hirsch explains it like this,

> Putting the imago Dei [image of God] first causes us to focus on the greater truths about any person. We move away from our preformed cultural assumptions, and from fixating on behaviors, to focusing on their innate potential to imitate their Creator. There is always the possibility of goodness and great beauty in all people. *Seeing* like this changes everything.[12]

To approach the world and each individual at each table this way means that all people, regardless of what table they sit at or what t-shirt they wear, reflect God and thus deserve to be treated generously.

Old Testament scholar Christopher Wright explains the significance even further, astutely highlighting how "image of God" takes priority over all the other labels. When we *start* with the theological truth that all people are created in God's image, he says we "must therefore treat all human beings with dignity, equality, and respect. When we look at any other person, we do not see the label (Hindu, Buddhist, Muslim, secular atheist, white, Black, etc.) but the image of God. We see someone created by God, addressed by God, accountable to God, loved by God, valued and evaluated by God."[13] How might the lunchroom dynamics change if that is how we first viewed people at other tables rather than as enemies or rivals?

Jesus, who was the *perfect* image of the invisible God (Col. 1:15; Heb. 1:3) and thus the model for how to treat others, repeatedly affirmed the image of God in every person. He did this by sharing tables, even with those others loved to hate (Luke 19:1–10). He did this by treating others with dignity, even those who viewed Scripture and worshiped differently from him (John 4:7–26). He did this by extending forgiveness to his enemies, even as they were in the process of killing him (Luke 23:32–38). Jesus didn't justify diminishing the image of God in others even when they were hated by the people, held a different theology, or made really awful choices (crucifying the Messiah being a classic "really awful choice"). Instead, Jesus chose the opposite. He called them to a better way, restored them to community, engaged them in conversation, and offered them mercy. All of those actions were rooted in a posture of generosity toward others.

Even though we live in a lunchroom permeated by the brokenness of Genesis 3, and even though we are *imperfect* image bearers, Jesus nonetheless expects his followers to model our posture after his. We see this expectation in one of Jesus' most famous teachings, the Sermon on the Mount, where he calls those listening to a posture that refuses to insult others, refuses to objectify people, refuses to treat one another as disposable, and refuses to return harm with harm, even to enemies (Matt 5:21–48).

For us, personally, few ideas have formed our theology and practice more than choosing to pay attention to the image of God in each and every person. Theologian and mystic Thomas Merton describes coming to a similar understanding during a sacred moment one day in his hometown of Louisville, Kentucky—a moment that changed him forever:

> In Louisville, at the corner of Fourth and Walnut, in the center of the shopping district, I was suddenly overwhelmed with the realization *that I loved all these people*, that they were mine and I theirs, that we could not be alien to one another even though we were total strangers. It was like waking from a dream of separateness, of spurious self-isolation in a special world ….
>
> This sense of liberation from an illusory difference was such a relief and such a joy to me that I almost laughed out loud …. I have the immense joy of being man, a member of a race in which God Himself became incarnate. As if the sorrows and stupidities of the human condition could overwhelm me, now that I realize what we all are. And if only everybody could realize this! But it cannot be explained. There is no way of telling people that they are all walking around shining like the sun.
>
> Then it was as if I suddenly saw the secret beauty of their hearts, the depths of their hearts where neither sin nor desire nor self-knowledge can reach, the core of their reality, the person that each one is in God's eyes. If

only they could all see themselves as they really are. If only we could see each other that way all the time.[14]

We don't think seeing each other as first and foremost created in God's image is an "if only" pipedream. We think it's a choice. A hard one, to be sure. And, as we said earlier, one that will take practice.

Once we prioritize seeing the image of God in others, it fundamentally changes how we view one another. We steward the "divine spark" in one another by "respect[ing], protect[ing], and honor[ing]" the image of God inherent in every person, especially when it is threatened.[15] Sometimes this threat is on a small scale—an impatient customer disrespecting a cashier. Sometimes the threat is on a much larger scale—the genocide of a people group. A generous way of seeing others insists that *any* threat to the divine image—in *anyone, anywhere*—goes against God's purposes. There is no place for a "that's not my problem" response, and certainly not for a "well, they deserve it because of X, Y, or Z" response because underneath all the differences is the same divine image.

Protecting the Flame

Imagine yourself at a birthday party.[16] It's the penultimate moment, just before the grand finale. And you—*you*—are in charge of lighting the candles and transporting the cake into the next room, while at the same time starting the "Happy Birthday" serenade with some semblance of being on key.

You light each candle carefully, placing your left hand under the cake platter, and then you slowly lift the cake to carry it to the one you are there to celebrate, who will then make a wish and blow out the candles. As you walk into the next room, almost without thinking, you raise your other hand and cup it sideways just in front of the combined flame of the candles. No one tells you to do this, but you know you must in order to protect the flame that burns because, even though fire is really strong, it is also extremely vulnerable. As author and speaker Rob Bell puts it when he compares the divine image to the flame of a candle: "This flame is incredibly robust, and … yet it's also fragile. It's strong, yet it's also shaky. It could burn down the house, and yet it's just sort of hovering there. There is limitless possibility in that flame and yet it must be carefully guarded."[17]

We need to recover our reflexive instinct to protect the divine flame that burns in each of us—the image of God. Our sorting into so many different lunch tables has led us to forget that we share the most important thing in common with all humanity: "God created humans in his image, in the image of God he created them" (Gen. 1:27). And so, if we want to be people who see others generously, if we want to be people who live faithfully in ACT V, if we want to move toward the way of Jesus in pushing the tables of this lunchroom together, we must relearn how to protect, respect, and honor the divine spark in others. Because *this* is where the story begins for every single one of us.

How to Build a Bar

If we were to make the table the most sacred object of furniture in every home, in every church, in every community, our faith would quickly regain its power, and our world would quickly become a better place. The table is the place where identity is born, the place where the story of our lives is retold, re-minded, and relived.

LEONARD SWEET

A few years ago, the Dutch brewing company Heineken produced a promotional campaign that puts another frame around this idea of being generous. Worlds Apart was a campaign "promoting openness and exploring whether common ground can unite people."[1] More a social experiment than a commercial, this four-and-half-minute film that has been viewed over 50 million times[2] introduces pairs of people who hold diametrically opposed views on various polarizing issues. Before filming, each participant knew nothing about the other or what the experiment involved.

The film shows each pair being tasked with assembling pieces of precut wood into a ten-foot-long bar top. In the process, they are asked to describe what it's like to be them in five adjectives and to name three things they have in common with their partner. Of course, these conversations do not yet expose their differences, only their similarities and points of connection.

After completing the assembly of the L-shaped bar, they are given bottles of Heineken (it was their commercial, after all) and a voice tells them to "Please stand to watch a short film." They watch pre-recorded inter-views that expose their partner's extreme opinions and attitudes, which starkly contrast their own views, be it on political, gender, or environmental issues. The tension is palpable as their partner's true identity is revealed, often through harsh and unforgiving words.

At that moment, the voice on the loudspeaker interrupts again and says, "You now have a choice. You may leave and be finished with this experiment, or you can stay and discuss your differences over a beer." As you would expect—given it's a commercial, not a reality show—the partici-pants choose to stay and deepen the bond they had begun to build with their partner despite their vast ideological differences. (Because, as we all know, beer will always win out!)

According to the creators, this commercial provoked a global conversa-tion driven by the belief that when you find a way to look past the labels and refuse to play the game, even the most divided people can come together for a conversation.[3] We absolutely agree. However, a generous posture may be easily created for advertising purposes but is much harder to pull off in real life.

Conversation Is Punished

In the ongoing search for a more generous lunchroom culture, there is a crucial yet often overlooked skill we need to be reminded of—how to have conversations. And, more specifically, how to have *generous* conversations.

Most of us have been piecing words together to form sentences since about eighteen months old, starting with "dad," "ball," and "mom." (Yes, much to the chagrin of the mothers who grew those babies for nine months, it seems many kids naturally prioritize their first words in that order.) But somewhere between learning to string words together and reflexively talking in fully formed sentences, we have forgotten how to have deep, meaningful conversations particularly with people who are different from us. Conversations that go deeper than, "How's it going?" or "How about the weather?" Conversations that can acknowledge and engage differences in ways that prioritize understanding over defensiveness. Conversations that value listening as much as speaking. Our echo chambers and hunkering-down approach have hindered our ability to have generous conversations, and it shouldn't take a beer commercial to show us that.

Trevor Noah, a comedian, writer, and former host of the American late-night talk program *The Daily Show* once shared how people had become less willing to participate as guests on his show: "I invite everybody on the show. People don't want to come. We live in a world where now having a conversation is punished, and I get it, people are afraid." He then describes how this shift happened in the mid-2010s:

> That's when I saw an immediate shift in where people were no longer interested. And also they no longer saw value in having a conversation with somebody else. They realized that no, if you just dug your heels in and entrenched you didn't have to justify your points of view. You just had to shout them really loud, and that was that.[4]

When our fears lead us just to turn up the volume on our opinions, we have the antithesis of generous conversations.

Our world is full of opportunities to shout out our points of view, most of which keep face-to-face conversations at a minimum. But if we are to push together our tables, something will have to change. Otherwise, we will only get further apart. What does our "therefore" look like in a world that has all but given up on the very idea of generous conversations?

Three Kinds of Conversations

Every conversation we have is influenced by all kinds of thoughts and emotions. Regardless of the subject or mode of communication, our approach to dialogue with others is determined by a range of desires and wants of which we are rarely cognizant. Journalist Charles Duhigg, in his book *Supercommunicators: How to Unlock the Secret Language of Connection*, concludes that when we take into account all the possible types of people and conversations and the ideas and problems we might discuss together, there are three basic kinds of conversations: "These three conversations—which correspond to practical decision-making conversations, emotional conversations, and conversations about identity—are best captured by three questions: *What's This Really About?*, *How Do We Feel?*, and *Who Are We?*" Each of these conversations ... draws on a different type of mindset and mental processing."[5]

Duhigg does a masterful job in unpacking the science of each of the three. But for our purposes—as we seek to engage in more generous conversations—the key aspect is learning to discern what type of conversation we are really having. Is it practical (*What's This Really About?*), emotional (*How Do We Feel?*), or about identity (*Who Are We?*)?

Are we being asked, "What should we do about the homeless situation in our city?" because this is a conversation that is searching for a *practical* answer to an overwhelming problem? Someone is looking for a solution that considers all the realistic and workable strategies for their homeless neighbors.

Or is this a discussion with stronger *emotional* ties? "My daughter was accosted on the street by one of those vagrants, so what is this city going to do about this issue of safety?" No solution is really being asked for; this is more about expressing anger and fear and the need for someone to empathize.

Or is this a question of *identity* because it's about how we relate to each other or society? "You need to know that I am on *this* side of the homeless issue ... or on *this* side ... and I want to know which side you're on, and if you're not with me, then I'm against you and everyone else who thinks like you."

A first step to more generous conversations is simply realizing that all conversations are not the same. If we're going to have better conversations, we need to understand what kind of conversation we are actually having. And to do that, we first need to learn the skill of asking more and better questions.

Stopping a Few Questions Too Soon

Since high school, my (Mark's) eldest son, Michael, has lamented his generation's inability to engage in generous conversation. He would often come to me confused and somewhat irritated: "I just don't think my friends understand what it means to have a real conversation. I ask them questions about themselves; I am genuinely interested, but that's the extent of the conversation. There is no back and forth. They simply don't know how to reciprocate. They never ask anything back. Ever. I know everything about them; they know nothing of me. They are just not very curious."

David Brooks estimates "that only 30 percent of the people in the world are good question askers. The rest are nice people, but they just don't ask. I think it's because they haven't been taught to and so don't display basic curiosity about others."[6] No doubt there are a multitude of reasons for our lack of conversational skills. Regardless of the causes, the results are contributing to an increasing inability to talk to each other—to have deep and generous conversations where we pay attention to what the other person says rather than to our phones. This growing phenomenon stems from our lack of curiosity and our inability to ask more and better questions while being genuinely interested in the responses that follow. Too often we stop conversing or redirect to another shallow topic before we ever get to anything of substance. What if we took the time to ask the one or two more questions that would bring about a more meaningful conversation?

In his book *How to Know a Person,* David Brooks makes a distinction between two ways people approach the art of conversation:

In every crowd there are Diminishers and there are Illuminators. Diminishers make people feel small and unseen. They see other people as things to be used, not as persons to be befriended. They stereotype and ignore. They are so involved with themselves that other people are just not on their radar screen.

Illuminators, on the other hand, have a persistent curiosity about other people. They have been trained or have trained themselves in the craft of understanding others. They know what to look for and how to ask the right questions at the right time. They shine the brightness of their care on people and make them feel bigger, deeper, respected, lit up.[7]

To have generous conversations is to illuminate and not diminish, to be deeply curious, to ask just one more question. It is realizing that we are not in a conversation to win the argument or to persuade someone to come to our side of an issue; we refuse to play the game and instead come with a posture of generosity in the hope of learning and understanding more, even if we don't agree. It is choosing to take one step toward pushing tables together with someone from the other side of the lunchroom.

Barbeque Sauce

If we are to develop a generous posture and form relationships that go beyond the surface, the way forward must involve not just *more* questions but *deeper* questions.[8] Questions that dig below the surface, beyond discussions about the weather and how bad the referees were last night and cost our team the game. More than the shallow questions that you would answer on any form in any doctor's office—address, place of employment, marital status, how often you drink alcohol, what medicines you're taking.

We need to find ways to inquire about someone's values, beliefs, and hopes and dreams for their family or community—questions that deepen relationships in a way that the question, "So, did you see it's supposed to storm tomorrow?" never will. Questions that require more than a yes or no answer. Questions that uncover memories or motivations—"You're in med school; what makes you want to do that? Was there a doctor in your past that inspired you to pursue this? Where do you see the greatest need in the medical profession?" In a world of shallow questions, we need to find ways to explore the deeper ideas that don't naturally arise. To do so is a refusal to stay at surface-level conversations and prevents us from maintaining our comfortable and unquestioned seats at our same old tables.

A powerful example of deep curiosity fueling generous conversations can once again be found in our mustached, corn-fed, barbeque-eating Kansan-turned-AFC-Richmond coaching guru, Ted Lasso. In what has become a quintessential scene from the show, Ted is playing a game of darts in the local pub against the villainous Rupert. Just before Ted's last throw, he is told he needs two triple 20s and a bullseye to win (evidently, an almost impossible achievement in darts). Rupert sarcastically chides his rival, "Good luck," with no expectation that Ted will beat him with a near-miraculous three-shot score.

Ted responds, "You know, Rupert, guys have underestimated me my entire life. And for years, I never understood why. It used to really bother me. But then one day, I was driving my little boy to school, and I saw this quote ... and it was painted on the wall there. It said, 'Be curious, not judgmental.' I like that."

Ted calmly throws his first dart, hitting a triple 20.

He continues, "So, I get back in my car, and I'm driving to work, and all of a sudden it hits me. All them fellas that used to belittle me, not a single one of them were curious. You know, they thought they had everything all figured out. So, they judged everything, and they judged everyone. And I realized that their underestimating me ... who I was had nothing to do with it. 'Cause if they were curious, they would've asked questions. You know? Like, 'Have you played a lot of darts, Ted?'"

And with his second dart, he hits another triple 20.

"To which I would've answered, 'Yes, sir. Every Sunday afternoon at a sports bar with my father, from age ten until I was sixteen when he passed away.'"

Ted looks at Rupert, then back at the dartboard, and pauses dramatically. As if uttering the words to inspire him to victory, he stares at the target and says, "Barbecue sauce," before planting his final dart directly in the bullseye as the crowded pub goes wild.[9]

To return to Brooks' terminology, Rupert was a Diminisher, not an Illuminator. He assumed he knew all he needed to know about Ted. To "be curious, not judgmental," on the other hand, is the epitome of generosity. It doesn't assume but instead seeks to understand. This ability to suspend judgment and pursue curiosity is at the heart of what it means to really see people, as we proposed in chapter ten. If we don't first *see* someone generously, *conversing* with them generously is nearly impossible. But when we ask one or two more questions, we realize that maybe the tables in the lunchroom aren't as far apart as we thought.

The Lost Art of Looping

Good listening is essential to generous conversations. As social researcher Hugh Mackay explains, "When we listen, we are being remarkably generous: we are offering the other person the gift of understanding; the gift of acceptance (even if not agreement); the gift of taking that other person seriously."[10]

In his book *Life Together*, pastor Dietrich Bonhoeffer traces the divine origins of listening, echoing Jesus' prayer in John 17. He writes,

> The first service one owes to others in the community involves listening to them. Just as our love for God begins with listening to God's word, the beginning of love for other Christians is learning to listen to them. God's love for us is shown by the fact that God not only gives us God's word, but also lends us God's ear. We do God's work for our brothers and sisters when we learn to listen to them.[11]

Though Bonhoeffer writes specifically about "love for other Christians," we believe, as followers of Jesus, we should apply this principle more broadly to those at *all* tables in the lunchroom—whether they are Christians or not.

Most people rarely struggle with the ability to speak but are not nearly as gifted at listening, especially to those at *other* tables. Often—especially when we know disagreement is imminent—we reflexively, almost subconsciously, stop listening when the other person begins to speak and instead start to prep our rebuttal in our mind even before they finish. We are just waiting for our chance to respond. It's not hard for someone with a different ideology than ours to recognize that we've stopped listening and that we're just waiting for our turn to prove them wrong. And, more often than not, they then reciprocate our response. The result is that neither side ever hears the other.

Duhigg explains this negative reciprocity and provides what we consider to be a generous solution. He calls it "looping for understanding." Because of our listening inadequacies and our default defensive and combative responses, he suggests that what is most important in our conversations is not just listening but *proving* we're listening. There are three steps to looping for understanding, according to Duhigg. The *first* enacts our latent curiosity—just ask a question. (Preferably, this should be a deep question, but really any question will work. Just make sure that it is not an argument hidden in a question.) Then simply listen to what the person says in response. "*Step two* is repeat back in your own words what you just heard them say. Show that you heard them and show that you processed it. And then the *third step*, and this is the one people usually forget, is ask if you got it right."[12]

Duhigg explains that reciprocation is hardwired into all of our brains, which means that if we've proved to someone that we have listened to them, the other person will want to listen back. If we learn to listen carefully and generously, we'll find that we are much less likely to be formulating our responses to what we have heard.

To engage in the art of looping is to attempt to bring generosity to our conversations. It is not to multiply our shallow discussions, nor is it to be used to argue our point. Instead, we can grasp a bit of how others, even those at other tables, view the world, which allows us to "draw the connection between the thing we care about and the thing they care about."[13] And that might be cause enough to break out a Heineken.

Posture over Position

Another tool essential to practicing the art of generous conversations is a willingness to *prioritize posture over position*. Pastor and author Eugene Peterson, who passed away in 2018, embodied this idea throughout his life. In Peterson's authorized biography, *A Burning in My Bones,* Winn Collier masterfully details Peterson's approach to the growing divisions he witnessed and experienced in his world as an author and pastor, especially in the last few years of Peterson's life.

"Abandoning the idea of rigid perfection allowed him a certain nimbleness. There may even be occasions when what was *pastorally* needed may not be what was *theologically* preferred,"[14] Collier writes of Peterson's posture, further describing it as both "generous" and "unanxious."[15] Peterson displayed an intellectual humility, recognizing that "dexterity and attentiveness" were required more than rigid theological positions shouted from on high. Speaking about this tension, Peterson remarked, "I live in company with Pentecostals and Presbyterians, Republicans and Democrats, evangelicals and schismatics—I am their pastor, not their policeman."[16]

In what reads as a lament, Peterson said: "How the so-called Christian community can generate so much hate is appalling. Haven't we learned anything about civil discourse? Will we ever? And it is so debilitating—we have this glorious gospel to proclaim and give away and we gang up against one another and throw dogma-rocks."[17] Peterson's approach opened him up to what he referred to as a "barroom brawl with the sheriffs out in full force."[18] Especially in the last few years of his life, Peterson lived in a sometimes strained place in the evangelical world due to his commitment to fostering generous conversation by infusing wisdom and humility in his interactions with others, regardless of whether his conversation partners reciprocated that generosity.

Listening to others and their differing ideas can feel like a somewhat dangerous approach in a lunchroom that seems to lack all forms of generosity. Approaching conversations and aspiring to adopt a posture of intellectual humility requires us to speak three simple words with regularity: "I don't know." This would be, as John Pavlovitz writes,

> A welcome sound to the people who comprise the Church. It would be life-giving to the frustrated faithful trying to navigate the paradox of the spiritual journey, the tension of holding belief and doubt with equal vigor. What people in the seats and the pews so desperately desire are leaders who are willing to be vulnerable, who will give voice to the question, who will give them permission to be unsure, who will make space at the table for their own vacillation.[19]

Generous conversations often contain that most welcomed phrase to those at other tables in the lunchroom. Those three simple words, "I don't know," can bring with them disdain and contempt but are crucial if we are to be generous in our conversations. They indicate that we are surrendering to the belief that all we know is not all there is.

Saying "I don't know" is not just a willingness to admit our lack of understanding on a matter; it is also the ability to acknowledge that the other person might be right and that we might be wrong. Former governor of Tennessee, Bill Haslam, was once asked how faith informed his politics. In response, Haslam recounted the counsel he received from his mentor— Howard Baker, a former US senator: "Always assume that the other fella might be right."[20] Responding to this insight, theologian Lee Camp writes,

> The idea is to begin simply with the possibility that I may be wrong, even about some of my most cherished convictions. This posture allows me to release my death grip on my defensiveness and assume that the truth will not be assisted by my contempt, condescension, or anger toward those who disagree with me. This posture trusts that, among people of good-will, there is much to be gained by open and honest discourse about our differences.[21]

This "assuming the other fella might be right" isn't just a theoretical posture for Haslam; it's something he lives out. Since 2022, Haslam (a Republican who served eight years as governor) has come alongside Democrat Phil Bredesen (another two-term governor of the state) to cohost a podcast aptly named *You Might Be Right*. This podcast tackles the most divisive political issues by fostering civil conversations between people with opposing views. Though "the big sort" would indicate that these men with opposing affiliations should be shouting at each other from different tables, instead they have pushed tables together. In doing so, Haslam and Bredesen exemplify how generous conversations can transform the dynamics of the lunchroom.

The popularity of this podcast reveals a yearning for models of generous conversations, where people refuse to play the same old lunchroom games. To take on the posture of nimbleness, dexterity, and attentiveness with an unanxious posture requires the ability to admit we not only don't know the answer to all the world's problems but also that we may be wrong about anything we think we know. It requires that we pay more attention and ask different and better questions. And this posture of intellectual humility, as we generously converse with one another, just might be the ingredient we need to lead us to a very important "superpower."

Invisibility or the Ability to Fly?

It always prompts a fun discussion at a dinner party: *If you could have any superpower, what would it be?* The answers are usually far-ranging. Most involve some supernatural ability that would give us an advantage or control over people or laws of physics. (For what it's worth, the funniest answer to the "superpower question" that I [Mark] have ever heard came from my son, Matthew, who was eight or nine years old at the time and declared boldly, "My superpower would be the ability to control ceramic tile!" We have yet to understand the significance of that answer.)

Business leader Vala Afshar once said that "to strongly disagree with someone and yet engage with them with respect, grace, humility, and honesty, is a superpower."[22] We're not sure exactly what costume would be appropriate for such a superhero, but we fully concur with Afshar's idea. Learning the art of conversing with that level of generosity could possibly get us our own Marvel movie. (You must admit, there are weirder super-heroes out there).

It's worth noting that Afshar's quote doesn't imply that resolution is the end goal of engaging in a disagreement. Generous conversation is not about *conflict resolution*; it is about engaging in conflict, as he said, with respect, grace, humility, and honesty. Learning to be curious, asking that question, and practicing the art of looping are not just steps toward the ultimate goal of resolution. Generous conversation does not have sameness as its goal, nor is it about simply tolerating the other. Generosity means giving space and invitation amid our differences to any other person from any other table because they are created in the image of God.

Contrary to what one might think, *conflict* is not the villain this super-power must battle to the death. Instead, our Lex Luthor, our nemesis, is our shallow, immature, divisive responses to conflict and disagreement. Barbara Brown Taylor describes recent shifts in our rhetoric and postures toward one another, even those closest to us: "Words that were not always loaded are loaded now. People who were not always defensive are defensive."[23] She goes on to describe her surprise at how natural it was for her to skewer a family member over their differing political views at a social gathering:

> Two years ago I savaged a young relative of mine when he started ragging on my failed presidential candidate. We had never had any reason to lay down rules of engagement before. We had never had any practice. In the heat of the moment, the imbalance in power never even occurred to me. I just blew up. When I had finished twirling my fire batons at him, it was hard to say who was more burned. He seemed unable to move. I seemed unable to apologize. *I was there when this boy was born,* I thought. If I couldn't do better than that, wasn't it time to give Jesus my resignation.[24]

Somewhere along the way, we have learned to view disagreement as antithetical to the ways of Jesus. We're not so sure it is. Jesus' approach to tables wasn't predicated on agreement or the absence of conflict. Jesus had his fair share of both disagreement and conflict, sometimes even at the table.[25] Generous conversation is not the elimination of disagreement but finding a way to normalize it and package it in a superpower casing of respect, grace, humility, and honesty.

Remarkable Things Can Happen

As we mentioned in chapter one, I (Mark) was incredibly fortunate to have the opportunity to lead the planting of a church we called Crossings in downtown Knoxville in 2007—a church where Heather has now also been a leader for over a decade. The name of our church is derived from the story of Jacob recounted in Genesis 32. Jacob had a somewhat sordid and convoluted relationship with much of his family and with God. After crossing the River Jabbok one night, Jacob anxiously anticipates meeting with his estranged brother Esau the next day. Left alone, Jacob subsequently wrestles all night long with a character most believe to be God.

At the end of this nighttime wrestling match, Jacob holds tightly and demands to be blessed by his opponent. This demand comes from someone who had already received quite a diverse list of blessings (some obtained dishonestly and some by the grace of God). It was as if he was still working out life, faith, and blessing, which we believe is much of what the wrestling was about.

As a faith community, Crossings tries to be incredibly clear that we believe every one of us should be given the opportunity to cross the River Jabbok, a place to wrestle with questions of faith and a space for generous conversation with people who don't always agree with each other and who can grapple with notions of faith together. We desire to be a community that learns to disagree generously, giving space to each other. When we describe those who are a part of our faith community, we try to be transparent so that those inquiring about our take on the most recent cultural topic or political issues can understand how we might respond. Over the years, we've often said something like: "There are people here who believe *this* way on an issue and those who believe *that* way on that same issue. What you will hopefully find is a faith community that will be generous with each other in our differences. If you are looking for a place where everyone is going to have the same opinions and beliefs as you do on every political, social, and theological issue ... well [*and we say this as kindly as possible*], let us help you find another community that will be more aligned with what you're looking for."

In the next chapter, we will dig a bit deeper into what it means to be generous in our gatherings; but it's important to acknowledge the differences that already exist in faith communities. If those differences are there—and they are—pretending that everyone agrees on every theological, ethical, political, and social issue is misguided at best and harmful at worst. It alienates those who do believe differently or those who are still trying to figure out what they believe. And if we fail to create spaces for generous conversation and instead make uniformity on every one of those issues the criterion for belonging, we'll find that we're actually creating more tables rather than pushing them together.

Crossings has struggled and wrestled, like Jacob with Yahweh, to cultivate a superpower that embodies respect, grace, humility, and honesty. As Barbara Brown Taylor writes, "When people figure out that unity is about more than agreeing with each other and reconciliation has more to do with staying in the room than with winning—then remarkable things can happen."[26] We agree with Taylor—a generous posture in our conversation, if we're willing to adopt it, just might be the superpower that starts to change the lunchroom.

More Picnics

*A church, when it is working, is one of the loveliest things there
is, and the sense of the presence of God and of the presence
of Holy Spirit and the love of Jesus in that community—
rooted in the sacraments, meeting around scripture, getting
on with the job in the world—this is what it's all about.*

N. T. WRIGHT

More picnics.

THE DALAI LAMA, UPON BEING ASKED HOW
TO PROMOTE GLOBAL PEACE

"The way we gather matters." That's the opening line of Priya Parker's book *The Art of Gathering: How We Meet and Why It Matters*. Parker, who trained in group dialogue and conflict resolution, has experience working with race relations at universities in the US and peace processes worldwide, including the Arab world, southern Africa, and India. Let's just say the woman knows how to encourage people to work together despite their differences! Although her focus isn't on churches, her job of helping groups "to collectively think, dream, argue, heal, envision, trust, and connect for a specific larger purpose" sounds exactly like what the church needs to be doing.[1]

Parker argues that though how we gather matters, "most of us spend very little time thinking about the actual ways in which we gather…. We spend much of that time [in various gatherings] in uninspiring, underwhelming moments that fail to capture us, change us in any way, or connect us to one another."[2]

Transforming the lunchroom to align with Jesus' vision more closely begins by adopting a generous posture in the way we see each other and in the conversations we have. But we believe there is another significant step we must take if we are to change the lunchroom at a much deeper level. And so, as we near the end of this book, we believe a final "therefore" relates to *how* we gather.

Whether it's a church gathering, a work meeting, a neighborhood BBQ, a conference call over Zoom, or a small dinner with friends around the table, every gathering has the potential for a deeper connection, a community that goes beyond superficiality and small talk to real connection—a belonging that transforms us. *How* we cultivate community matters; *how* we gather matters.

Why We Gather

Before getting to *how* to gather, Parker encourages us to reflect on *why* we gather. More specifically, why do followers of Jesus gather—both in corporate church settings and in other informal ways? Now, some Christians might say, "because we're supposed to" or "because that's what we've always done." Although those answers aren't wrong, they're far from satisfying. We don't go on an anniversary date with our partner "because we're supposed to" or "because that's what we've always done." If those were our only motivating factors, that time together wouldn't do much to transform our partnership.

So why *do* we gather? Before you read on, we'd encourage you to attempt to answer that question yourself—why do followers of Jesus gather? Why do you (or don't you) gather regularly with the people of God? Are your answers to those questions meaningful and fulfilling or simply the responses that are expected of Christians? Do you—do *we*—need better answers?

Consider for a moment why the original improvisers—who transformed from a small group of Jews in Judea to hundreds of thousands of people with varying ethnicities and backgrounds across the Roman Empire—gathered as they did. They didn't gather to become a new religion. They didn't gather because of programs that met their every need. They didn't gather because they had fancy new buildings, cutting-edge music, or a charismatic pastor with 100,000 Instagram followers. So then, why? Why did gathering become a part of this thirty-year movement that changed the world?

We believe it had much to do with these earliest followers of Jesus finding a place to belong in a fractured lunchroom. They gathered because it gave them an identity and a new way of life.

A new way of life that insisted that wholeness and restoration for all was God's original intent and that brokenness would not have the last word (Gen. 1–2).

A new way of life that said everyone—especially the one you least expected—was invited to the table because the Master wanted his table to be full (Luke 14).

A new way of life that cared for each other's spiritual, physical, and financial needs (Acts 2–6).

A new way of life that was willing to consider the renewed ways that God was working in the world and respond faithfully to what they witnessed (Acts 10, 15).

A new way of life that was willing to have the hard conversations and find a way forward together (Acts 15).

A new way of life that said the old, the young, the men, the women, the Jews, the Samaritans, the Greeks, the rich, the poor, the slaves, the free, the single, the married, the widowed, the sexual others were all welcomed and wanted (Gal 3:28, and, well, the whole book of Acts).

A new way of life that was so committed to its central conviction—that Jesus was the fullest revelation of God—that all other secondary issues stayed in their proper secondary places and resulted in a unity that was so compelling, so other-worldly, that people wanted to be a part of this movement that was changing the world (John 17).

This "new way of life" that emerged from their new identity was their *why* of gathering.

And it should be ours.

Refining Our Why

This new identity, one we share with the early followers, explains the "why" of our gathering. We, too, gather to affirm our identity. We, too, gather to give witness to this new way of life. But there are other reasons why we gather that impact *how* we gather.

We gather corporately to hear the Word of God proclaimed and to celebrate the communion meal that reminds us of the great acts of God in the world. This proclamation and this table orient us to the larger story of God we are a part of.[3] They teach and remind us who we are (God's beloved creation, created in his image) and what our mission is (to join God's mission of healing the brokenness in our fractured world).

We gather to worship God in community. Yes, we can and should worship God anytime and anywhere—hiking in the mountains, rocking a fussy baby to sleep, or sitting in traffic on our commute home from work. But setting aside a time and place to worship God *with others* reminds us that we are not on this mission alone. It orients us away from ourselves and toward God and others.

We gather to encourage and be encouraged by others. When our faith (or our bodies, finances, or marriages) is strong, we hold up our brothers and sisters who are weak. When our faith (or our bodies, finances, or marriages) is weak, we let our brothers and sisters who are strong hold us up.

We gather out of a hunger for relationships, out of a desire to cure the tragic disease of loneliness, and to quench our thirst to be a part of something that is bigger than ourselves.

All these reasons, among others, lay behind our various gatherings. Although it is absolutely crucial that our Sunday corporate gatherings are characterized by generous spaciousness, those gatherings alone are not enough. We should be pursuing generosity in *all* our ways of gathering. In the city and county where we (both Mark and Heather) live, an area supposedly somewhere near the heart of the Bible Belt in the US, 79 percent of people are not gathering in churches on Sundays.[4] (We assume that number is much higher in almost every other context). Yet many church leaders are endlessly assessing how we can make a better gathering for the 21 percent who *do* gather on Sundays. But when was the last time we sat and strategized and asked questions about how to make the way we gather with those 79 percent of people more meaningful?

And so we ask: How might we make all our gatherings—our churches, our families, our neighborhoods—into spaces of abundant generosity and belonging that allow each of us to become more like Jesus and encourage us to honor the divine spark in one another?

Wells Not Fences

We both grew up in the Midwest—central Indiana for Mark and northwest Ohio for Heather. One thing these two places have in common, besides their abundance of corn, is that they are *flat*. Really flat. Kansas-flat. Flat-earthers-should-move-their-headquarters-to-one-of-our-hometowns flat. In addition to corn, both places have their fair share of farm animals. In such rural farming communities with flat land, most farmers build fences to keep their animals in and other animals out. Though neither of us claims to be expert fence-builders (literally or metaphorically), we're pretty sure if we *did* want to build a fence, we'd want the land to be flat.

In other farming communities, where the land is not as flat and easy to build on, farmers still need to care for their livestock. Around the countryside of rural England, for example, where the terrain is rugged or rocky, building fences to contain sheep or cattle just isn't feasible; it's next to impossible. So what do these farmers and shepherds do instead? Instead of building fences, they dig deep wells, trusting that their animals will never wander too far away from that which gives and sustains life.[5]

We worry that over-explaining this metaphor might diminish its power, not unlike having to explain the punchline of a joke, and yet this metaphor has been deeply formative for our understanding of how we gather generously. Jesus is the well. Period. He is the one who gives life to all. All other commitments pale in comparison to this. So rather than constructing fences to keep certain folks in or other folks out, a community that is generous in how it gathers recognizes that its job is to lead people to the well—Jesus— instead of policing the borders to determine who's in and who's out.

Missiologists Michael Frost and Alan Hirsch are worth quoting at length here, as they explain how a wells-not-fences approach (what they call a "centered" set,[6] in that it's centered around Jesus) isn't a free-for-all in terms of belief or practice. Instead, it is a humble acknowledgment that no one has arrived, and we're all trying to move closer to Jesus, the One who gives and sustains life. Frost and Hirsch write:

> Since at the core of a centered set is Christ, a church should be concerned with fostering increasing closeness to Jesus in the lives of all those involved .... A centered-set church is not concerned with artificial boundaries that bounded-set churches have traditionally added. In bounded-set churches all sorts of criteria are determined for the acceptance or rejection of prospective members (smoking, drinking alcohol, living together outside marriage, differing views on Christ's return). In a centered-set church it is recognized that we are all sinners, all struggling to be the best people we can be. But we also believe that the closer one gets to the center (Christ), the more Christlike one's behavior should become. Therefore core members of the church will exhibit the features of Christ's radical lifestyle (love, generosity, healing, hospitality, forgiveness, mercy, peace, and more), and those who have just begun the journey toward Christ (and whose lives may not exhibit such traits) are still seen as "belonging." No one is considered unworthy of belonging.... *Belonging is a key value.*[7]

When our focus is on Jesus, in whom we find life-sustaining water, our focus remains on *his* vision for the lunchroom. When we recognize that everyone is on the journey toward Jesus (a *generous view of each other* that grants that people have faith journeys that can look drastically different), we can then engage our differences in healthy ways (*generous conversations* that respect others' views and are open to learning new things), which in turn results in a *generous gathering,* where each person has space to wrestle, to consider others' views, to change their mind, and to grow in Christlikeness.

What Do We Do When Everyone Is Thirsty?

In the 2016 film adaptation of Rudyard Kipling's *The Jungle Book*, a poignant scene unfolds around a small watering hole. A tall, jagged rock formation known as the Peace Rock, emerges only during the severest of droughts, when most of the jungle's water has evaporated. As the water recedes and the rock is exposed, it signals the water truce, when all animals in the jungle come to the Peace Rock because it is the only place where they can find water. The animals are forbidden from hunting and killing each other at the river bank next to the rock because, as the narrator explains, "By law of the jungle, drinking comes before eating, so you could come to the Peace Rock on a day like this and find *all* people side by side."[8] This water-truce scene shows porcupines mingling with antelopes, peacocks strutting beside rhinos, and even mice scurrying alongside the feared panther Bagheera. All are gathered at the Peace Rock—none threatened by the other's presence—because they recognize that getting to the water is crucial for their existence. Without it, nothing else matters.

The Peace Rock is simply another frame for wells not fences. When there's only one water source, when we're in a religious drought (which might be an apt way to describe the current religious landscape in many places across the West),[9] people need to be willing to come side by side, keeping their differences *in perspective*. (Notice we didn't say *denying their differences*.) The water is more important than whether the animal has four legs or two, whether they're carnivores or herbivores, whether they're Republican or Democr ... sorry, whether they're nocturnal or diurnal. Water is the most important thing. When we keep Jesus' vision for the lunchroom as our primary focus, when it becomes our Peace Rock, we gain perspective, and that perspective changes how we gather. And so we ask: As followers of Jesus, are we willing to come to our own water truce and be a model of the Peace Rock in the midst of a spiritual drought?

Reordering the Bs

When it comes to issues of belonging, many churches have tradition-ally relied on a model that requires either shared belief or adherence to specific behaviors. When a person meets the church's standard for belief and behavior, *then* they can belong. The model goes "Behave → Believe → Belong," and in this model, belonging is conditional. This model asserts the gospel is for all but predicates belonging on thinking and acting a certain way. You can only pull up a chair if you behave and believe like we do.

Wheaton professor Mark Yarhouse, a clinical psychologist who specializes in conflicts between a person's religious and sexual identity, instead advocates for a missional model akin to "wells not fences" that changes the order of the Bs. Rather than Behave → Believe → Belong, the model for gathering goes Belong → Believe → Become. This model of the lunchroom generously pulls up a chair for someone—regardless of what table they come from—and trusts that an identity with this new way of life will be transformative.

Of course, this way of gathering is messy and, if we're honest, can be a bit awkward sometimes.[10] When belonging comes first, you have people in all different places who gather, some far away from the well, some closer. Some who gather have positive feelings about faith, the church, or both; they've been supported and loved and have a meaningful story of faith. Others have negative feelings about one or both; they've been on the receiving end of the abuse of power or exclusion and hurt. Many have mixed feelings—they're trying to hold onto faith as tightly as they can but have been accused of doubt, questioning, or not having enough faith. Still others are hopeful—maybe there *is* a better way than what they've seen or heard, a community that is trying to do more than simply lecture or entertain.

We love the vision that author Rachel Held Evans proposes in her memoir on the complexity of being part of a faith community: "Imagine if every church became a place where everyone is safe, but no one is comfortable."[11] *Safe*—if we learn the basics of generous gathering, then any group assembled can act as a Peace Rock where no one's vulnerabilities or differences are exploited; getting to the water to drink is the most important thing. But not necessarily *comfortable*—since no one has "arrived" at perfect wholeness, we all have blind spots, weaknesses, and brokenness that need healing and transformation. We're more likely to become aware of our own needs for repentance if we're in a community with people different from us. When we're in close community with someone in a different income bracket, with someone of a different race, with someone who votes differently, with someone who was raised with a different view of the Bible, we're able to recognize that maybe we don't have it all figured out, that maybe we haven't taken Jesus' teaching on wealth very seriously, that maybe our preferred candidate isn't quite as aligned with the values of the kingdom of God as we wanted to believe.[12] And these realizations are only likely to happen in the midst of a generous community.

A generous community requires a leadership that is humble and vulnerable enough to admit they don't know everything about everything and might even be wrong sometimes. A generous community requires people who are okay with difference, even when—especially when—that difference is uncomfortable (presidential election years, anyone?). A generous community requires a generous view of others and generous conversations, both of which require grace, forgiveness, humility, and a willingness to keep fighting for Jesus' vision for the lunchroom, even when it's hard, even when our feelings are hurt, even when we feel misunderstood. A generous community requires a commitment to listening to how God is working in others' lives, sometimes in ways that might be different from our own, and, like the apostle Peter, being willing to change our minds. A generous community helps us to discern together how to faithfully improvise, balancing what it is to be faithful to the story so far while having enough faith to follow the Spirit's leading into what's ahead. A generous community requires an endless supply of folding chairs (perhaps literal, definitely metaphorical) that can always be pulled up to squeeze a few more people around the table.

Collective Moments of Joy and Pain

Remember The Three Ds of Disconnection from chapter three—distance, distortion, and distrust? These are the opposite of generous gathering, the opposite of community. In her research on belonging, Brené Brown found that an antidote for disconnection was to "show up for collective moments of joy and pain so we can actually bear witness to inextricable human connection."[13] Many of us have experienced this at various times in our lives. It's human instinct to want to share our deep joy or sorrow with others.

I (Mark) live in the greatest neighborhood in the world. It's not up for debate. I will gladly fight anyone who doubts me. It's a relatively small neighborhood in the city, around ten city blocks of homes. Since moving here over a decade ago, my wife, Monica, and I have gotten to know most of our neighbors through book clubs, ice cream socials, garden tours, Christmas dinners, sharing lawnmowers, and summer backyard picnics where over a hundred people will gather to feast.

From the day we moved in, we became really good friends with our neighbors across the street, Steve and Terry. They had lived in the neighborhood for almost twenty years and had been together for over five decades. Between conversations on the boulevard, marveling at one another's latest home improvement, and sharing countless dinners, we learned their story and came to love our dear neighbors.

Two years ago, at the age of eighty-two, Terry was diagnosed with prostate cancer. It was incredibly hard to watch cancer ravage the body of our once-active friend. Although he never lost his infinite quirkiness or sense of humor, we missed seeing him outside working on one of his many projects or hearing about the latest collectibles he and Steve had purchased at one of the dozen yard sales they had stopped at that morning. (Terry collected all sorts of oddities, but my favorite was his arrangement of vintage thermostats throughout the house.)

Ten months after his cancer diagnosis, Terry passed away peacefully at home. Instead of a funeral just after his passing, Steve planned a memorial to celebrate Terry's life. However, to allow the out-of-town family to attend, it was scheduled a few weeks after his death.

Because we loved and knew him so well, the sadness of losing Terry engulfed our neighborhood as a collective grief, and I began to wonder if there might be a way to gather and remember Terry sooner than later—a way to meet up and share in this great loss. I remembered learning about the Jewish mourning ritual of "sitting *shiva*," which is a seven-day period where family members of the deceased gather and mourn the passing of their loved one together in community.[14] While being conscious of cultural appropriation and not wanting to take ownership of a tradition that wasn't mine, I still thought that this beautiful Jewish practice of creating space in our community to sit together in our grief was something from which we could learn.

And so Monica and I put out word that we were opening our home to come together, to remember and share stories about our dear, dear friend Terry. Many in the neighborhood quickly responded, bringing food, drink, and a host of stories. We ate together and then squeezed as many people as possible into our living room. I explained the idea of this spiritual practice of sitting in our grief with one another, and then for the next hour or so, our neighbors grieved, mourned, and laughed as we celebrated Terry's life. From Steve sharing the story of their life together, to tale after tale of Terry's sense of humor, his gentle spirit, and his ability to infuse creativity into every aspect of life, these neighbors, from age five to ninety-five, gathered in a truly generous way. (By the way, my role in this was not as a pastor but as a neighbor who missed his friend. The last thing I wanted to be in that situation was the pastor or leader in charge of a "service.")

In the two years since Terry's death, many have spoken about the significance of that specific gathering. The memory is usually followed with the phrase, "We just live in the *best* neighborhood." In fact, recently, when our friend Maggie, who lives four houses down, died suddenly of a heart attack, some of the neighbors responded almost immediately with, "We need to do that thing we did when Terry died. Let's get together and bring food and tell stories about Maggie." And we did. And it was beautiful. And I'm sure we will do it again and again—it seems to have become a permanent part of our very special neighborhood culture.

There is something generous about gathering for "collective moments of joy and pain." Finding ways to show up with purpose, meaning, and great love for each other, regardless of our differences, is a powerful way of pushing the lunchroom tables together.

Too Good to Be True?

In the summer of 2021, our church in Knoxville had recently begun meeting in person again after the COVID-19 outbreak over a year earlier. As we shifted from gathering on Zoom to gathering in person, we spent several weeks reflecting on what it meant to gather. All questions were being considered—who, why, how? Just like every other community after the global pandemic, we were not the same as we were a year prior. Some people had left; others had joined. We were all a bit nervous about what the new talking points and dividing lines meant for our community—we'd seen what masks, vaccines, social distancing, and school closures had done to discourse online and within our families. How would those issues impact our gathering? Was there any hope for a community to transcend division and embody unity in the midst of difference?

One Sunday, a balmy southern summer day, our community gathered at Christenberry Elementary School, as we had done so many times over the years. Some folks were masked and keeping their distance, while others were unmasked and joyously embracing friends they hadn't seen in months. As laughter filled the air, Mark told the story of Mephibosheth.[15]

Mephibosheth was the son of Jonathan, who was the son of Saul, thus making Mephibosheth the grandson of the first king of Israel. In 2 Samuel 4:4, we learn about this young man with a mouthful of a name: "Saul's son Jonathan had a son who was crippled in his feet. He was five years old when the news about Saul and Jonathan came from Jezreel. His nurse picked him up and fled, and in her haste to flee it happened that he fell and became lame. His name was Mephibosheth." In case your Old Testament history is rusty (we get it, really), here's a little of the backstory. Jonathan and King David were best friends. In one story, Jonathan even saved David's life when Jonathan's father, Saul, was trying to kill him. (The family drama in 1 and 2 Samuel makes *The Sopranos* seem tame.) In response, David promised Jonathan that he would always take care of his family should something happen to him (1 Sam. 20:15–16).

Spoiler alert: Something did happen to Jonathan (and to King Saul, too). Both were killed in battle, and the throne was left to David. Although

David had no intention of harming Saul's family (1 Sam. 24:21–22), Saul's family didn't necessarily know or trust that. Kings were sometimes known for executing rivals to their throne, even within their own families.[16] That fact, along with the fact that Saul had tried to kill David multiple times, makes it likely that Saul's family feared for their safety when David became king. So, when they learned that Saul and Jonathan had both been killed, the servants of Saul's family packed up quickly and hurried to escape. In their rush, we learn that a nurse tragically dropped five-year-old Mephibosheth, leaving him crippled.

Jonathan's family managed to escape to Lo-debar (a city up north that means "barren place"), but no doubt Mephibosheth grew up asking why he was different from the other kids. Perhaps his nurse told him something like this: "Well, if it weren't for David, we wouldn't be in this place. And if it weren't for David, you wouldn't be crippled. *He's* why we're here. *He's* why this happened to you." We imagine Mephibosheth grew up fearing and maybe even hating David.

As David's kingdom prospered, he remembered the promise he had made to his best friend. He asked his servant whether anyone in Saul's family was still alive so that he could show God's kindness to them for Jonathan's sake. His servant responded, "There remains a son of Jonathan; he is crippled in his feet" (2 Sam. 9:3). David asks, "Where is this son?" Almost every other reference to Mephibosheth mentions that he's "crippled," but David, for some reason, stays away from the label.

As we know well, the lunchroom is all about labeling. We've all had the misfortune of being labeled, and we've probably labeled others, too. We're so good at it, so quick to classify others. Divorced. Alcoholic. Failure. Unemployed. We love our labels.

But David, the one in the position of power, refused to label Mephibosheth and instead invited him to his palace. When Mephibosheth arrived, he fell on his face and honored the king, rendering his service to David. But David assured him, "Do not be afraid, for I will show you kindness for the sake of your father Jonathan; I will restore to you all the land of your grandfather Saul, and you yourself shall eat at my table always" (2 Sam.

9:7). Mephibosheth had to be thinking, *This can't be right. Isn't this the guy that caused so many problems for my family? Surely this is a trick.* He had to be thinking that such unexpected generosity and hospitality were too good to be true.

What was Mephibosheth's reaction to David's reassurance? He *again* prostrated himself before the king, proclaiming his unworthiness to have a seat at the table: "What is your servant, that you should look upon a dead dog such as I?" (2 Sam. 9:8). He had been labeled for so long that he bought into the labels himself. His circumstances had nearly extinguished his flame.

But David ignored Mephibosheth's labels and declared that everything that had belonged to Saul, he was now returning to Mephibosheth. He then resoundingly proclaimed, "Mephibosheth shall always eat at my table" (2 Sam. 9:10). This person—dropped, crippled, whisked away to hide in fear for his life—would now be treated with the generosity and grace befitting a grandchild of the king. From then on, he ate at David's table, as if he were one of the king's own sons.

David's family was large, and his children were well-known throughout the kingdom. In addition, he had many powerful people who could eat at his table, and now Mephibosheth would be joining them. Charles Swindoll describes what the nightly scene might have looked like at this king's dinner table:

> The meal is fixed and the dinner bell rings and along comes members of the family and their guests. Amnon, clever and witty, comes to the table first. Then there's Joab, one of the guests—muscular, masculine, attractive, his skin bronzed from the sun, walking tall and erect like an experienced soldier. Next comes Absalom. Talk about handsome! From the crown of his head to the soles of his feet there is not a blemish on him. Then there is Tamar—beautiful, tender daughter of David. And, later on, one could add Solomon as well. He's been in the study all day, but he finally slips away from his work and makes his way to the table.
>
> But then they hear this clump, clump, clump, clump, and here comes Mephibosheth, hobbling along. He smiles and humbly joins the others as he takes his place at the table as one of the king's sons.[17]

In a room with the potential to resemble any lunchroom anywhere, David—a recipient of a similar generosity throughout his story— offered a different table, a better table. He gave Mephibosheth what he had quite possibly been searching for his entire life: a table at which to sit—where the only label applied was that of "son"—and a gathering place where he could finally belong and find an identity with a new way of life.

As our community gathered there that evening at Christenberry Elementary School, Mark transitioned from the story of Mephibosheth to the story we transition to every week—the story of the table, the story of the bread and the wine. We had spent over a year taking the bread and wine individually in our living rooms separated by computer screens. But that day, we continued to do what we'd done every week since Crossings' beginning; we did what followers of Jesus have done every week since the church's beginning. In all our types of brokenness, amidst all the differences that had seemed to multiply in the previous year, we gathered around a table of belonging to proclaim our identity in Jesus and with this beautiful, shared way of life.

Called to Something Better

When we look at the story of God, we see God creating *all humans* in his image. We see God blessing Abraham and his descendants so that *all the families of the earth* could be blessed. We see Jesus, the great descendant of Abraham, God incarnate, casting a vision where *all* have a seat at his table. We see him casting a vision of *unity* and commissioning his disciples to make disciples *to the ends of the earth*, and we see them following those instructions, proclaiming that Jesus is Lord *of all*. They welcome Jews, Samaritans, Gentiles, widows, eunuchs, males, females, and folks with language barriers to the table, all the while proclaiming that those identities are subsumed under the greater identity of being "in Christ." When we read this beautiful story, we refuse to believe that God accepts the labels we so readily pass out, the tables we so quickly assign to those who look or believe or act differently than we do.

Jesus has called us to something better, a more generous way of being in the lunchroom with a different kind of table—a table for those who have no other table; a table for those who are done with the labels; a table for those who are tired of there being so many damn tables, each with their own rules and power dynamics and fears.

Can we build a better lunchroom?

A lunchroom whose motto is, "There's still room at the table," and that's always willing to pull up another chair.

A lunchroom that's fiercely committed to welcoming those with their backs against the wall.

A lunchroom where we've crumpled up our "never-never" lists and thrown them in the trash next to the empty milk cartons.

A lunchroom where people are always working on faithful improvisation, where they're fiercely committed to the story that came before but not afraid to say "Yes, and" to bring the story closer to its completion.

A lunchroom that's known for its generous way of seeing others and its generous conversations and generous ways of gathering.

Can this happen?

We think so, because, well, it's never too late to be who you—who we—might become.

Epilogue

A More Beautiful Way

Do not try to satisfy your vanity by teaching a great many things.
Awaken people's curiosity.
It is enough to open minds, do not overload them.
Put there just a spark.
If there is some flammable stuff, it will catch fire.
ANATOLE FRANCE

"Do you have a sense of where Christianity might be headed?" the interviewer asked author and former pastor Brian McLaren. "And do you see signs of hope that something more transformative and life-giving might be emerging?"

After a thoughtful pause, McLaren responded:

> I expect that Christianity will become uglier than it's ever been in our lifetimes in the next ten years. *And* I expect that more beautiful expressions of Christianity will be emerging than we've ever seen in our lifetimes. Because I think the two go together: As the ugly becomes uglier, more and more people will wake up and say, *I don't want to be part of this; I can't be part of this.* And many of them will then dare to start rethinking, and when that happens, new possibilities will emerge.... I think you should say, *Things will get better, and things will get worse. And I am going to try to invest my life where they're getting better. And I'm going to be aware that that might involve deep rethinking on my part.*[1]

Over the last few years, our experiences as pastor, professor, and authors have forced us to grapple with the very same question of Christianity's future; living with this uncertainty is partly what motivated us to write this book. In the previous twelve chapters, we've aimed to set before you both the troubling realities that fracture our world (the ugly) and the hopeful vision of wholeness offered by Jesus (the beautiful). As followers of Jesus empowered by the same Spirit who birthed a movement that changed the world, we all have the opportunity to shape the future of Christianity. We get to influence how this story is told and how it is lived out. The degree of beauty or ugliness is directly related to our engagement with the story of God and our commitment to faithfully improvise in accordance with the radical ways of Jesus.

We hope that all of us might embody "more beautiful expressions of Christianity," expressions that understand the deep social and theological origins of our fractured world, that embrace our part to play in the larger story of God, and that aspire to be generous in how we see each other, talk with each other, and gather with each other. Foundational to this hope is the belief that it's never too late to be what we might become. By asking different questions and being willing to learn new things, we want to pursue a better way to live in the lunchroom. We are called and commissioned to something bigger than ourselves: to push the tables together, to invite and make room for *every* person, and to pursue a vision for oneness with God and each other that Jesus said could change the world.

Try Something

We realize that what we propose in this book won't be easy. Acknowledging the desperation so many of us feel at the current state of the lunchroom is painfully uncomfortable, and trying to actually transform the lunchroom into Jesus' vision will be extremely difficult. Our world will resist it. Many churches may even resist it. But we must do something.

In 1932, in the throes of the Great Depression, two years before becoming the US president, Franklin D. Roosevelt challenged the graduating seniors at Oglethorpe University with these words:

> The country needs and, unless I mistake its temper, the country demands
> bold, persistent experimentation. It is common sense to take a method
> and try it: If it fails, admit it frankly and try another. But above all, *try
> something*.... We need enthusiasm, imagination, and the ability to face
> facts, even unpleasant ones, bravely.... Yours is not the task of making

your way in the world, but the task of remaking the world which you will find before you. May every one of us be granted the courage, the faith, and the vision to give the best that is in us to that remaking![2]

Rejecting the current way of living in the lunchroom and instead trying to embody Jesus' way will require courage, faith, and vision. Without them, there may be no way forward toward the more beautiful way. And so, we implore you: Above all, try *something*.

Don't Call It a Conclusion

I (Mark) have never been a fan of the concept of a *conclusion*. I've always felt that a well-crafted book doesn't need a grand ending that presents the reader or listener with the proverbial final word on a subject with no room for further discussion. Instead, a book should linger in our minds, prompting questions and sparking conversations long after we turn the last page. It should be the first word, not the last.[3] A good book invites you to journey and explore a mystery that the words on the page simply set in motion.

Our goal in this book has been to be honest about the current state of the lunchroom and to help imagine what could happen if we take Jesus' ideas and the faithful improvisation of the early church further and deeper. We believe that if someone leaves a teaching or a sermon with all the answers to their questions, we haven't done our jobs well. But if they leave with more questions than answers and a desire to *learn* something new, *try* something new, and *become* something new, then we've succeeded. This book is no different. Although it concludes here, the story is far from over. May these last pages be the first pages of the next conversation about a new kind of lunchroom where the tables are pushed together, and Jesus' prayer in John 17 becomes our reality.

So, go ahead.

Write the next page.

Have the next conversation.

Pull up the next chair.

Have the courage to try *something*.

Choose the beautiful over the ugly.

Acknowledgments

Heather

So many people have left their fingerprints on this book, and it is better for it. First, many thanks to the students in my spring 2024 Acts and the Mission of God class at Johnson University, who read early drafts of the Acts content in the book and helped me think better about faithful improvisation in our world today. Special thanks to Jonathan Kelley for his detailed feedback on early drafts.

I never imagined I would end up with such an embarrassment of riches when it comes to friendships in Knoxville, but I have truly learned what the phrase "women supporting women" means as I wrote this book. Kristi, Jamie, Chantele, Katie, Brittany, Rachel O., Maria, Molly, Lauryl, Rachel H., Jen, and so many others—the way y'all show up for your people is such a gift. Thank you for all the ways you cheered me on.

To my family in Ohio—the Maases, Cramners, and Gormans: I care about Jesus so deeply because of the faith you gave and helped sustain in me. Your commitment to the work of the church is a large part of why I wanted to write a book *for the church.*

Above all, I am grateful for the love and support of my husband, Jamey, and our daughters, Anna and Elise. Jamey, no one believes in my work like you do, and there's no one in the world I'd rather have in my corner than you. Thank you for your steady encouragement and empowerment. Anna and Elise, I hope one day you read this book and it makes you proud. May you grow up to be women who push tables together and who always choose generosity toward others.

Finally, Mark: Thank you for asking me to write this book ... twice! I have learned so much from you about storytelling, the creative process, and, most importantly, how to follow Jesus in a life-giving community. The Crossings community you built has been one of the greatest gifts to my faith.

Mark

As always, the deepest of thanks to the *best person I know*, my wife of thirty-seven years, Monica. No one believes in me more and cheers me on to kingdom-of-God things in my life. This book wouldn't have been written without you.

To my dearest friend and mentor, Jim Schmotzer: The journey we have shared over the past decades has brought to life in me so many things that Heather and I have attempted to bring to life in this book. And all it took was to approach it one bird at a time. Shalom.

Thanks to the many church leaders who are a part of Three Rivers Collaborative. Your spirits of generosity, curiosity, and collaboration truly inspire me. As we all work together to follow Jesus in Knoxville, each of you continues to give evidence that the ideas of this book are actually possible in the day-to-day lives of so many different kinds of faith communities.

And to my brilliant coauthor, Heather—that em dash and these exclamation points are just for you!!! It has been an absolute joy writing this book with you. I'm forever grateful for your willingness to join together and to wrestle with and bring to fruition a work that is so much better because of that collaboration. Thank you for being willing to work so incredibly hard with great joy toward an end product that will hopefully play a role in pushing more and more tables together. Your relentless passion for Jesus, the Scriptures, and the church are at the very core of this book.

Heather and Mark

First and foremost, our deepest gratitude goes to Anna Robinson, our editor. Anna, from the very beginning you believed in this book and have invested so much in it. Few people possess both the literary and theological acumen you do, and our work is so much better because of your involvement. Thank you, thank you, thank you.

To the entire 100 Movements Publishing team—especially Brenna Varner and Helen Bearn: Your eagerness to help, your expertise, your patience with queries and requests, and your enthusiasm for this book—we're in your debt for all of it.

Maddie Tate, we are so grateful for all your behind-the-scenes work in bringing this book to completion. You were a sounding board, a researcher, and, most of all, an encourager. And you never once complained when your meetings got moved because our storyboarding and editing always took longer than we anticipated. Thanks for everything!

Johnson University, you have been a gift to both of us for many years and in many ways. We could fill pages with the names of folks who helped with the book specifically and with encouragement in life and ministry more generally. We hope this book honors Johnson's commitment to deep theological work in service of the church.

Shalom.

Notes

1 Walking in Shoes Too Small

1. Anne Lamott, *Bird by Bird: Some Instructions on Writing and Life* (New York, NY: Anchor Books, 1995), 34 (emphasis original).

2. *Mean Girls*, directed by Mark Waters, written by Melanie Mayron (2004; United States: Paramount Pictures), film.

3. See High School Musical Cast, "Stick to the Status Quo," by David Lawrence and Faye Greenberg, recorded 2006, track 5 on *High School Musical*, Walt Disney Records.

4. Beverly Daniel Tatum, *Why Are All the Black Kids Sitting Together in the Cafeteria?: And Other Conversations About Race*, Rev. ed. (New York, NY: Basic Books, 2017), 132.

5. "Writers Speak; Lecture by James Baldwin on the Writer's Responsibility," New England Public Radio, American Archive of Public Broadcasting (GBH and the Library of Congress), Boston, MA, and Washington, DC, accessed May 14, 2024, http://americanarchive.org/catalog/cpb-aacip-305-86nzshkq.

6. Ed Stetzer, "The 'Dangerous' Calling of Evangelical Ecumenism," ChurchLeaders, July 19, 2022, https://churchleaders.com/voices/429768-the-dangerous-calling-of-evangelical-ecumenism.html (emphasis original).

7. Stetzer, "The 'Dangerous' Calling of Evangelical Ecumenism" (emphasis original).

8. John Pavlovitz, *A Bigger Table: Building Messy, Authentic, and Hopeful Spiritual Community* (Louisville, KY: Westminster John Knox, 2017), 38.

9. Frederick Buechner, *Now and Then: A Memoir of Vocation* (San Francisco, CA: HarperOne, 1991), 20.

10. https://crossingsknoxville.com.

11. https://threeriverscollaborative.com.

12. For an excellent history of this faith tradition, see Richard T. Hughes and James L. Gorman, *Reviving the Ancient Faith: The Story of Churches of Christ in America*, 3rd ed. (Grand Rapids, MI: Eerdmans, 2023). This may look like a shameless promotion of my (Heather's) husband's book, but I genuinely recommend it as an excellent analysis of both the contributions of and the challenges facing the Stone-Campbell Movement.

13. Rob Bell, *What We Talk about When We Talk about God* (New York, NY: HarperOne, 2014), 153–73.

14. David Brooks, *The Second Mountain: The Quest for a Moral Life* (New York, NY: Random House, 2019), xxiii.

2 Assessing the Fracture

[1] Brené Brown describes the frustration we feel when we can't articulate our emotions: "We feel hopeless or we feel a destructive level of anger." We believe the same can be said when we don't have appropriate explanations for our experiences. Brené Brown, *Atlas of the Heart: Mapping Meaningful Connection and the Language of Human Experience* (New York, NY: Random House, 2021), xxi.

[2] Bill Bishop, *The Big Sort: Why the Clustering of Like-Minded America Is Tearing Us Apart* (Boston, MA: Houghton Mifflin, 2008), 6. For specific examples of these trends, see pp. 7–8.

[3] Brené Brown, *Braving the Wilderness: The Quest for True Belonging and the Courage to Stand Alone* (New York, NY: Random House, 2017), 51. For more details on the data between 1992 and 2016, see Gregor Aisch, Adam Pearce, and Karen Yourish, "The Divide Between Red and Blue America Grew Even Deeper in 2016," *The New York Times*, November 10, 2016, https://www.nytimes.com/interactive/2016/11/10/us/politics/red-blue-divide-grew-stronger-in-2016.html.

[4] Bishop, *The Big Sort*, 13, 15 (emphasis added).

[5] Bishop, *The Big Sort*, 12.

[6] We admit that the terms "conservative" and "liberal" may be too misunderstood to be helpful, not only because different groups often use the terms to mean different things, but also because they mean different things when applied to religion and politics. Nonetheless, we use them here because Bishop talks about politics and faith together using these labels, though whether that's out of a lack of precision or because he recognizes that religious and political commitments are often bound up together, we're not sure. His observation uses both religious and political categories: "We discovered that people who left counties with large numbers of Evangelicals rarely moved to counties dominated by Democrats." Bishop, *The Big Sort*, 12.

[7] Bishop, *The Big Sort*, 12.

[8] Bishop, *The Big Sort*, 14.

[9] Cass R. Sunstein, "The Law of Group Polarization," *John M. Olin Program in Law and Economics Working Paper* 91 (1999): 1–39.

[10] Cass R. Sunstein and Reid Hastie, *Wiser: Getting Beyond Groupthink to Make Groups Smarter* (Boston, MA: Harvard Business Review Press, 2015). In his chapter, "The Psychology of the Tribe," Bishop also reaches this conclusion: "There have been hundreds of group polarization experiments, all finding that like-minded groups, over time, grow more extreme in the direction of the majority view." See Bishop, *The Big Sort*, 67.

[11] Sunstein and Hastie, *Wiser*, 77–88.

[12] Sunstein, "The Law of Group Polarization." Cf. Bishop, *The Big Sort*, 68–69, for a summary of various social psychological theories on these dynamics of group polarization.

[13] Bastian Berbner, *In Search of Common Ground: Inspiring True Stories of Overcoming Hate*

in a Divided World, trans. Carolin Sommer (New York, NY: The Experiment, 2022), 175. He quotes this study: Solomon E. Asch, "Effects of group pressure upon the modification and distortion of judgments," in Harold S. Guetzkow, *Groups, Leadership and Men: Research in Human Relations* (Pittsburgh, PA: Carnegie Press, 1951), 177–90 (emphasis added).

14 David French, "Does Ideology Shape Community or Community Shape Ideology?" The Dispatch, September 6, 2022, https://thedispatch.com/p/does-ideology-shape-community-or.

15 Brown, *Braving the Wilderness*, 47.

16 Matthew S. Vos, *Strangers and Scapegoats: Extending God's Welcome to Those on the Margins* (Grand Rapids, MI: Baker Academic, 2022), 6.

17 Vos, *Strangers and Scapegoats*, 7.

18 Vos, *Strangers and Scapegoats*, 8.

19 Sunstein and Hastie's explanation of how confidence, extremism, and corroboration by others are linked is worth quoting in full: "When people lack confidence, they tend to be tentative and therefore moderate, knowing that their own views may be wrong. The great American judge Learned Hand once said 'the spirit of liberty is that spirit which is not too sure that it is right.' Tentative people respect the spirit of liberty. But as people gain confidence, they usually become more extreme in their beliefs. The reason is that a significant moderating factor—their own uncertainty about whether they are right—has been eliminated. With respect to group polarization, the key point is that agreement with others tends to increase confidence and through that route, to increase extremism. It is partly for this reason, then, like-minded people, having deliberated with one another, become surer that they are right and thus more extreme. In many contexts, people's opinions turn extreme simply because their views have been corroborated and because they become more confident after learning that others share their views. Groups can blunder badly in this way." See Sunstein and Hastie, *Wiser*, 84–85.

20 Brown, *Braving the Wilderness*, chapter four.

21 Brown, *Braving the Wilderness*, 65.

22 Michelle Maiese, "Dehumanization," Beyond Intractability, July 2003, https://www.beyondintractability.org/essay/dehumanization. Cited in Brown, *Braving the Wilderness*, 72.

23 Brown, *Atlas of the Heart*, 234 (emphasis original).

24 George Carlin, "George Carlin—Idiot and Maniac," YouTube video, June 21, 2012, https://www.youtube.com/watch?v=XWPCE2tTLZQ.

25 Skye Jethani makes this point about the disciples as he discusses how fear drives so much of the culture wars, particularly how groups get mad when other people aren't afraid of what they are. See Phil Vischer and Skye Jethani, "The War on Winsomeness and Interfaith Cooperation," in *Holy Post Podcast*, May 18, 2022, https://www.holypost.com/post/episode-509-the-war-on-winsomeness-interfaith-cooperation-with-eboo-patel.

26 Brown, *Braving the Wilderness*, 51.

27 Brown, *Braving the Wilderness*, 136–37.

28 *Star Wars: Episode I—The Phantom Menace*, written and directed by George Lucas (1999; United States: 20ᵗʰ Century Fox), film.

29 Jonathan Haidt, "Why the Past 10 Years of American Life Have Been Uniquely Stupid," *The Atlantic*, April 11, 2022, https://www.theatlantic.com/magazine/archive/2022/05/social-media-democracy-trust-babel/629369/.

3 Moving the Tables: An Origin Story

1   In 2:24, the uniting "as one flesh" is a reference to sexual relationships, but the larger principle applies to humanity and their relations at large.

2   While the conversation appears to be between the serpent and the woman, Gen. 3:6 states clearly that she gave the fruit "to her husband, *who was with her*, and he ate" (emphasis added).

3   Burton L. Visotzky, *The Genesis of Ethics: How the Tormented Family of Genesis Leads Us to Moral Development* (New York, NY: Crown Publishers, 1996), 9.

4   Much of the material in this section is informed by Phyllis Trible, *Texts of Terror: Literary-Feminist Readings of Biblical Narratives* (Philadelphia, PA: Fortress, 1984), 9–35.

5   *The Breakfast Club*, written and directed by John Hughes (1985; United States: Universal Pictures), film.

6   Theologian Miroslav Volf describes this move poignantly: "Why do we hate others or turn our eyes from them? Why do we assault them with the rhetoric of inhumanity? Why do we seek to eliminate, dominate, or simply abandon them to their own fate? Sometimes the dehumanization and consequent mistreatment of others are a projection of our own individual or collective hatred of ourselves; we persecute others because we are uncomfortable with strangeness within ourselves. Others become scapegoats, concocted from our own shadows as repositories for our sins and weaknesses so we can relish the illusion of our purity and strength." See Miroslav Volf, *Exclusion and Embrace: A Theological Exploration of Identity, Otherness, and Reconciliation*, Updated edition (Nashville, TN: Abingdon, 2019), 131.

7   Wilda C. Gafney, *Womanist Midrash: A Reintroduction to the Women of the Torah and the Throne* (Louisville, KY: Westminster John Knox, 2017), 40. Gafney contends that even Hagar's name is a testament to her status as "other": "Hagar's *otherness* is at the heart of her portrayal in the Torah, Tanakh and New Testament. Her name, I have contended, is not *her* name. *HaGar* means 'the foreigner,' 'alien,' or 'sojourner' in Biblical Hebrew. The alien is one who resides in the land that is not their own, as Abraham's family residing in Canaan as aliens, and the familiar protections in the Torah for the aliens in the midst or gates of the Israelites. It strains credulity to imagine an Egyptian mother naming her child 'alien' in the language of the people to whom she will be subjected in servitude, and not just because *HaGar* is masculine in Hebrew."

8   Walter Brueggemann, *Genesis*, Interpretation (Louisville, KY: John Knox, 1982), 151;
     Gerhard von Rad, *Genesis*, trans. John H. Marks, Old Testament Library (Philadelphia,
     PA: Westminster, 1956), 186.

9   On the power dynamics involved in this exchange as they relate to patriarchal law
     see Delores S. Williams, *Sisters in the Wilderness: The Challenge of Womanist God-Talk*
     (Maryknoll, NY: Orbis, 2013), 20–21.

10   Renita Weems describes the promotion and demotion of Hagar like this: "As quickly
     as Hagar was elevated to the position of wife in her mistress' house, she was reduced
     back to the position of slave. She, who had been to Abram as a wife through a transfer
     of power, once again became property—again, without her permission. Once Sarai's
     authority over the pregnant slavewoman was restored, the barren wife proceeded to
     punish the slavewoman for humiliating her." See Renita J. Weems, *Just a Sister Away:
     A Womanist Vision of Women's Relationships in the Bible* (San Diego, CA: Publishing/
     Editing Network, 1988), 6.

11   Trible, *Texts of Terror*, 13. See Trible's larger chapter on Hagar on the many parallels
     between Hagar's story and the Hebrew slaves' story in Exodus, including how both flee
     from their oppressors (Sarai and Pharaoh). See also Gafney, *Womanist Midrash*, 44.

12   For various theological interpretations of this instruction (i.e., God directing a slave
     to return to oppression), see John Goldingay, *Genesis*, Baker Commentary on the Old
     Testament (Grand Rapids, MI: Baker Academic, 2020), 266–67.

13   Trible, *Texts of Terror*, 17; Gafney, *Womanist Midrash*, 42.

14   In Genesis 17:1–16, when God announced to Abram that circumcision would be the
     sign of the covenant, he also changed Abram's name to Abraham and Sarai's to Sarah.
     We follow that name change here in how we refer to the characters.

15   Williams notes that Sarah's future well-being depended on Isaac's (and Hagar's on
     Ishmael's): "Among these ancient Hebrews, wives could not inherit their husband's
     wealth. Therefore, neither Sarah nor Hagar would inherit anything from Abraham
     should they outlive him. The responsibility for Sarah's sustenance and care would
     ordinarily fall upon the firstborn son as chief inheritor of his father's wealth. But if
     the firstborn, Ishmael, also becomes head of the family and/or tribe, Sarah may have
     considerably less power and status than she has as a wife of Abraham and as she would
     have as mother of the son who inherited the larger share of the wealth and therefore
     power. Needless to say, Isaac would have considerably less wealth, power and status as
     brother of the firstborn." See Williams, *Sisters in the Wilderness*, 25.

16   Frederick Buechner, *Beyond Words: Daily Readings in the ABC's of Faith* (New York, NY:
     HarperOne, 2004), 143.

17   Trible offers a stunning parallel between Hagar and the suffering servant of Isaiah 53:
     "This Egyptian woman is stricken, smitten by God, and afflicted for the transgressions
     of Israel. She is bruised for the iniquities of Sarah and Abraham; upon her is the chas-
     tisement that makes them whole." Trible, *Texts of Terror*, 28.

18   Trible, *Texts of Terror*, 28.

[19]   For helpful scholarship on Jewish people in the context of Roman Hellenism (various sects, movements, beliefs, etc.), see Archie T. Wright, "Jewish Identity, Beliefs, and Practices," in *The World of the New Testament: Cultural, Social, and Historical Contexts*, eds. Lee Martin McDonald and Joel B. Green (Grand Rapids, MI: Baker Academic, 2013), 310–24.

[20]   For a succinct essay summarizing key characteristics of these groups during Jesus' time, see Daniel R. Schwartz, "Jewish Movements in the New Testament Period," in *The Jewish Annotated New Testament*, eds. Amy-Jill Levine and Marc Zvi Brettler, 2nd ed. (Oxford, UK: Oxford University Press, 2017), 614–19.

[21]   On the historicity of the antagonistic Jewish claims about Samaritans as "syncretistic semipagan neighbors," see Lidija Novakovic, "Jews and Samaritans," in *The World of the New Testament*, eds. McDonald and Green, 207–16. She urges us not to accept antagonistic presentations of the Samaritans in Jewish sources uncritically. John may highlight the more extreme tension between the groups when he claims "Jews do not share things in common with Samaritans" (John 4:9; cf. Josephus), but those don't represent all Jewish-Samaritan relationships, which may not have been that tense. Such expressions nonetheless show us how at least some ancient Jews viewed Samaritans.

[22]   Amy-Jill Levine, *Short Stories by Jesus: The Enigmatic Parables of a Controversial Rabbi* (New York, NY: HarperOne, 2014), 104–11 (quote from p. 104).

[23]   Howard Thurman, *Jesus and the Disinherited* (Boston, MA: Beacon Press, 1996), 83.

[24]   On estimated percentages of the population living near, at, or below subsistence level, see David J. Downs, "Economics, Taxes, and Tithes," in *The World of the New Testament*, eds. McDonald and Green, 158–60.

[25]   David A. deSilva, *The Letter to the Hebrews in Social-Scientific Perspective*, Cascade Companions (Eugene, OR: Cascade, 2012), 105–6.

[26]   David A. deSilva, "Jews in the Diaspora," in *The World of the New Testament*, eds. McDonald and Green, 272–90.

4   To Roy's Question . . .

[1]   A story that places a character in an environment that is completely foreign.

[2]   Todd Spangler, "'Ted Lasso' Season 2 Delivers Biggest Premiere Audience for Apple TV Plus to Date, Company Claims," *Variety*, July 26, 2021, https://variety.com/2021/tv/news/ted-lasso-season-2-premiere-viewership-numbers-ratings-1235027673/.

[3]   Caroline Framke, "For Your Reconsideration: Ted Lasso," *Variety*, November 16, 2020, https://variety.com/2020/tv/columns/ted-lasso-season-1-jason-sudeikis-1234772230/.

[4]   Keri Lumm, "Ted Lasso is the Wholesome American Hero We Need," *Paste Magazine*, September 28, 2020, https://www.pastemagazine.com/tv/ted-lasso/ted-lasso-american-hero.

[5]   Lea Palmieri, "'Ted Lasso' is the Rare Show Every Human Can Enjoy," *Decider*,

October 8, 2020, https://decider.com/2020/10/08/ted-lasso-is-the-rare-show-every-human-can-enjoy/.

6   *Ted Lasso,* season 3, episode 12, "So Long, Farewell," written by Brendan Hunt, Jason Sudeikis, and Joe Kelly, directed by Declan Lowney, aired May 31, 2023, on Apple TV+.

7   *Ted Lasso,* season 3, episode 12, "So Long, Farewell."

8   My (Heather's) answer to this is much less profound. I'd pick the feeding of the five thousand because I love bread. I'd make sure I took a to-go box with me so the leftovers wouldn't go to waste.

9   Lesslie Newbigin, *The Light Has Come: An Exposition of the Fourth Gospel* (Grand Rapids, MI: Eerdmans, 1982), 223.

10 Newbigin, *The Light Has Come,* 235.

11 Marianne Meye Thompson, *John: A Commentary,* New Testament Library (Louisville, KY: Westminster John Knox, 2015), 357. Thompson writes, "A … characteristic of Jesus' prayer in John 17 is its orientation of the mission of God to the world. The term 'world' (*kosmos*) occurs 79 times in John, with almost half of those occurrences (38) found in chapters 14–17. Of those 38 uses, almost half (18) are found in this prayer. It is striking that as Jesus utters his final words to his disciples and prays for them, the world comes into such sharp focus."

12 Lindsey M. Trozzo, *Exploring Johannine Ethics: A Rhetorical Approach to Moral Efficacy in the Fourth Gospel Narrative,* WUNT 2 (Tübingen, Germany: Mohr Siebeck, 2017), 124 (emphasis original). For more nuance on how John uses the word "world" (*kosmos*), see pp. 166–67, where Trozzo explains that though the world often rejects God, it nonetheless "is the object of forgiveness, love, and life." Thus, rather than posing a threat to God's inclusive mission, it is the impetus for it.

13 Thompson, *John,* 280.

14 This is highlighted in John 12 when Jesus talks about the significance of his death: "And I, when I am lifted up from the earth, will draw *all people* to myself" (John 12:32, emphasis added). See Trozzo, *Exploring Johannine Ethics,* 155.

15 Some scholars rightly point out the contrast that John sets up between Nicodemus (a male insider who comes to Jesus at night) and the woman at the well (a female outsider whom Jesus approaches in the day). This might also lead readers to question Nicodemus's sincerity and response to Jesus. See, for example, Lindsey S. Jodrey, "The Woman at the Well: Commentary on John 4:1-42," Working Preacher, February 4, 2018, https://www.workingpreacher.org/commentaries/narrative-lectionary/the-woman-at-the-well/commentary-on-john-41-42. We think that contrast is helpful, *and* we think a charitable read is that he was looking to make room for another way of seeing the world or God, that he was searching for a new way of thinking and living, even if it took him a little while to figure out what that looked like. Such a read is at least somewhat warranted by the presence of Nicodemus at Jesus' grave. John 19:38–42 tells us that Nicodemus and Joseph of Arimathea cared for Jesus' body and prepared it for burial, suggesting that Nicodemus was willing not just to think differently but also to

let it transform his actions, even if it took him some time to get there. It reminds us of the theology of clicks from chapter one. This encounter with Jesus may have moved Nicodemus from a C to a D. Nicodemus still had a way to go to get to Z, but each click was a movement in the right direction.

[16]   With no offense to Higgins, who we think is one of the most underrated characters in the show. *Ted Lasso*, season 3, episode 12, "So Long, Farewell."

5   There's Still Room

[1]   Matthew Croasmun and Miroslav Volf, *The Hunger for Home: Food and Meals in the Gospel of Luke* (Waco, TX: Baylor University Press, 2022), 30 (emphasis added).

[2]   Commensality derives from the Latin terms *com* ("together with") and *mensa* (table).

[3]   Susanne Kerner and Cynthia Chou, "Introduction," in *Commensality: From Everyday Food to Feast*, eds. Susanne Kerner, Cynthia Chou, and Morten Warmind (London, UK: Bloomsbury, 2015), 1.

[4]   Eric D. Barreto, "A Gospel on the Move: Practice, Proclamation, and Place in Luke-Acts," *Interpretation* 72, no. 2 (2018): 178.

[5]   Barreto, "A Gospel on the Move," 178.

[6]   Barreto, "A Gospel on the Move," 178.

[7]   Robert J. Karris, *Eating Your Way Through Luke's Gospel* (Collegeville, MN: Liturgical Press, 2006), 14. Karris is not alone in observing this, but his work is especially accessible and a good synthesis of scholarship on the topic. For those wanting more on food in Luke, see his bibliography.

[8]   For a thorough engagement with primary sources on taxation in early Roman Palestine, see Fabian E. Udoh, *To Caesar What Is Caesar's: Tribute, Taxes, and Imperial Administration in Early Roman Palestine*, Brown Judaic Studies 343 (Providence, RI: Brown Judaic Studies, 2005). Of Udoh's many significant points, pertinent here is the observation that "there were, it would seem, no Roman tax collectors in the Jewish parts of the province of Judea. Tribute was collected by Jewish agents" (242). The two named tax collectors in the New Testament—Levi/Matthew (Mark 2:14; Luke 5:27–32; Matt. 9:9–13) and Zacchaeus (Luke 19:1–10)—are both Jewish.

[9]   Dominique DuBois Gilliard, *Subversive Witness: Scripture's Call to Leverage Privilege* (Grand Rapids, MI: Zondervan, 2021), 125. How representative Matthew and Zacchaeus were is up for debate. As New Testament scholar Mark Allan Powell notes, "Social-historical analysis of the ancient Near East has indicated that the great majority of tax collectors and prostitutes in Palestine at the time of Jesus were probably slaves." In other words, not all tax collectors or prostitutes had the ability to abandon their jobs for work that wasn't deemed sinful. Although Matthew and Zacchaeus did, others were trapped in a system where the exploited (enslaved people) were exploiting others (via over-taxation or bribes) to line the pockets of those higher up the food chain. And people hated them for it, even though many had no opportunity to leave because of

their enslavement. See Mark Allan Powell, "Table Fellowship," in *Dictionary of Jesus and the Gospels*, eds. Joel B. Green, Jeannine K. Brown, and Nicholas Perrin, 2ⁿᵈ ed., The IVP Biblical Dictionary Series (Downers Grove, IL: IVP Academic, 2013), 930. For more on the distinction between "chief" tax collectors and lower-level ones, see Luise Schottroff and Wolfgang Stegemann, *Jesus and the Hope of the Poor*, trans. Matthew J. O'Connell (Maryknoll, NY: Orbis, 1986), 6–13.

10 See Downs, "Economics, Taxes, and Tithes," 156–68, who describes how most inhabitants of the Greco-Roman world "lived at or near subsistence level" and whose lives were consumed by the struggle to survive. To be clear, these economic challenges were not only, or even primarily, from taxation; but exploitive taxation on top of other factors made a hard economic situation even harder. See Udoh, *To Caesar What Is Caesar's*, 286–87.

11 Gilliard, *Subversive Witness*, 126.

12 Barreto, "A Gospel on the Move," 180.

13 Joachim Jeremias, *New Testament Theology* (New York, NY: Scribner, 1971), 115–16. Quoted in Karris, *Eating Your Way Through Luke's Gospel*, 33. For other scholarly views on the significance of Jesus' table fellowship with sinners, see Powell, "Table Fellowship," 929–30, who summarizes Croassan, Wright, and Sanders.

14 To correct this misunderstanding, we cannot recommend this volume highly enough (we engage various essays from the volume in this section): Joseph Sievers and Amy-Jill Levine, eds., *The Pharisees* (Grand Rapids, MI: Eerdmans, 2021). We especially recommend Amy-Jill Levine's essay entitled "Preaching and Teaching the Pharisees," which addresses the urgent need for Christians not to misrepresent the Pharisees.

15 Josephus, *Ant.* 13.298; 18.15. Cited in Lawrence H. Schiffman, "Pharisees," in *The Jewish Annotated New Testament*, eds. Levine and Brettler, 622. The Pharisees, like many Second Temple Jewish groups, are difficult to reconstruct historically. Mark Allan Powell describes part of that challenge: "The letters of Paul usually are regarded as the only writings that we have from any Pharisee who belonged to what is called the Second Temple period of Judaism (515 BCE to 70 CE). True, the Roman historian Josephus claims that he was a Pharisee for a brief time (*Life* 2), but Paul was raised a Pharisee and continued to regard himself as a Pharisee throughout his entire life (Phil. 3:5). He remains an important figure for Jewish studies, though his ultimate identification with the Christian movement causes Jewish historians to question how truly representative a Pharisee he could have been (why didn't other Pharisees follow his lead or accept his arguments?)." Mark Allan Powell, *Introducing the New Testament: A Historical, Literary, and Theological Survey*, 2ⁿᵈ ed. (Grand Rapids, MI: Baker Academic, 2018), 251. The issue of how representative Paul is relates to the larger question of how to regard the New Testament's witness to the Pharisees in historical reconstructions considering the Gospels' sustained polemic against the Pharisees. On this topic, see Schiffman, "Pharisees," 620–21. See also the various essays in the "Historical Reconstruction" section of Sievers and Levine, *The Pharisees*.

16   Levine, "Preaching and Teaching the Pharisees," 403. These stereotypes of the Pharisees are not Levine's, of course; it's her description of what is sadly common in Christian teaching and preaching about the Pharisees.

17   Levine, "Preaching and Teaching the Pharisees," 419.

18   On the complex portrait of the Pharisees in Luke-Acts, See Hermut Löhr, "Luke-Acts as a Source for the History of the Pharisees," in *The Pharisees*, eds. Sievers and Levine, 170–84. He discusses whether Luke is more sympathetic to Pharisees than the other Gospel writers.

19   For more on Jesus' similarities with Pharisees, see Schiffman, "Pharisees," 621.

20   Powell, *Introducing the New Testament*, 42.

21   Mark Allan Powell, "Was Jesus a Friend of Unrepentant Sinners?: A Fresh Appraisal of Sanders's Controversial Proposal," *Journal for the Study of the Historical Jesus* 7, no. 3 (2009): 307. To those who assume the Pharisees' objections were related to ritual purity, Powell rightly points out, "The purity issue is never raised in reference to Jesus' eating with sinners, and our literature concerning tax collectors portrays them as dishonest crooks, not as people whose primary failings had anything to do with purity" (304). For other proposals on why the Pharisees might be upset over Jesus' fellowship with sinners, see pp. 302–6.

22   Amy-Jill Levine and Ben Witherington, *The Gospel of Luke*, New Cambridge Bible Commentary (New York, NY: Cambridge University Press, 2018), 387.

23   Levine and Witherington, *The Gospel of Luke*, 395.

24   Fred B. Craddock, *Luke*, Interpretation (Louisville, KY: Westminster John Knox, 2009), 177. Cf. Luke 6:34–45.

25   Cf. God as the host of banquets in Ps. 23:5; 30:9; 63:6; 65:5; 103:5; 132:15. John E. W. Watts, *Isaiah 1-33*, Rev. ed., Word Biblical Commentary 24 (Grand Rapids, MI: Zondervan Academic, 2018), 390.

26   Craddock is an outlier here. See Craddock, *Luke*, 179.

27   R. T. France, *Luke*, Teach the Text Commentary Series (Grand Rapids, MI: Baker, 2013), 249.

28   Levine and Witherington push back on an eschatological reading and a reading that views God as the host for a couple of (good) reasons. If God is the host, is God late in inviting the poor and blind, only after others reject him? Is God rejecting the Jews ("none of those who were invited will taste my dinner")? If it were the messianic banquet, there wouldn't be slaves or disabled, they point out, because "the messianic age is the time when all suffering, physical and economic, is ended" (399). These points are worth considering. Nonetheless, Luke 14:15 frames Jesus' story as eschatological by speaking of the kingdom of God in the future tense ("blessed is anyone who *will* eat bread in the kingdom of God," (emphasis added). Either way, it's about radical hospitality to those outside one's social circle—hospitality that treats them as equals, not just as objects of charity. See Levine and Witherington, *The Gospel of Luke*, 395–406.

29   Wilkins notes that Jesus' model of calling disciples to himself—i.e., the master taking

the initiative—deviated from the way that rabbis usually had disciples, which typically entailed the potential disciple approaching the rabbi and asking to study with him. See M. J. Wilkins, "Disciples and Discipleship," in *Dictionary of Jesus and the Gospels*, eds. Green, Brown, and Perrin, sec. 3.1.1.

30   Whether Simon was part of the revolutionary group known as Zealots or whether he was zealous in other ways (cf. Paul's self-description of his zeal manifesting in persecuting the church in Phil. 3:6) is debated in New Testament scholarship. Only Luke calls Simon a zealot (*zēlōtēs*). The other Gospel writers call him "the Cananean" (Matt. 10:4; Mark 3:18). Assuming Luke's use of Mark, as most scholars do, Luke deliberately changed Mark's "Cananean" to "zealot." Carroll notes the significance of this descriptor in Luke, who wrote after the Jewish rebellion against the Romans that resulted in the destruction of the temple: "Luke does not explain this epithet, but his audience looks back on the Zealot movement of the mid-60s C.E. that fomented rebellion in Judea and Jerusalem (see, e.g., Josephus, *J. W.* 2.8.1; *Ant.* 18.1.1, 6), resulting in catastrophic destruction to temple, city, and land. On the other hand, Paul is a self-described 'zealot for God,' according to Acts 22:3, and Simon, too, may be remembered for his religious zeal rather than his revolutionary leanings. Luke leaves the gap to be filled by the reader." See John T. Carroll, *Luke: A Commentary*, New Testament Library (Louisville, KY: Westminster John Knox, 2012), 142. For recent scholarship on Zealots, see James D. G. Dunn, "Prophetic Movements and Zealots," in *The World of the New Testament*, eds. McDonald and Green, 242–51. Dunn notes that even though the extremist faction didn't emerge until the time of the First Jewish Revolt, we can assume that Simon's zeal related to a deep commitment to only worshiping Israel's God. He adds, "That Jesus chose such an intensely religious person, possibly with strong political views about Rome's domination of Israel, is itself significant" (250).

31   Caleb Gilmore, "Cave. Table. Road—'A Risky Table,'" September 24, 2022, in *Crossings Knoxville*, podcast, 26:10, https://podcasters.spotify.com/pod/show/crossings-knoxville/episodes/Cave--Table--Road---A-Risky-Table-with-Caleb-Gilmore-e1nf7j7.

6   Yes, And

1   Emily Zemler, "15 Actors Who Went to Seriously Extreme Measures for a Role," *ELLE*, February 5, 2016, https://www.elle.com/culture/movies-tv/a33861/extreme-role-prep/.

2   Richard B. Woodward, "The Intensely Imagined Life of Daniel Day-Lewis," *The New York Times*, July 5, 1992, sec. 6.

3   *The Office*, season 2, episode 9, "Email Surveillance," written by Michael Shur, directed by Paul Feig, aired November 22, 2005, on NBC.

4   Basically any discussion of improv will discuss this maxim so it hardly needs citation, but we present to you what has to be the best title of an improv discussion ("Tina Fey's Rules of Improvisation That Will Change Your Life and Reduce Belly Fat*") by one of

the best improv actors of our time—Tina Fey. See Tina Fey, *Bossypants* (New York, NY: Reagan Arthur, 2011), 76–78.

5   "Don't Think Twice Clip—Rules of Improv," The Film Arcade, October 27, 2016, YouTube video, https://www.youtube.com/watch?v=0QW43wdbQwU.

6   He uses this specific term on p. 143 of *The New Testament and the People of God* and uses various similar terms in his other writings. He articulates his narrative hermeneutic in several of his writings, but the three that most informed this section are N. T. Wright, *The New Testament and the People of God* (Minneapolis, MN: Fortress, 1992), 139–44; N. T. Wright, *Scripture and the Authority of God: How to Read the Bible Today* (New York, NY: HarperOne, 2013), 121–27; N. T. Wright, "How Can The Bible Be Authoritative?," *Vox Evangelica* 21 (1991): 18–23.

7   Wright, "How Can The Bible Be Authoritative?," 25.

8   Wright, *The New Testament and the People of God*, 140.

9   Wright, *Scripture and the Authority of God*, 123.

10 For a history of the name of the book, see Christopher R. Matthews, "Acts of the Apostles," in *The Oxford Encyclopedia of the Books of the Bible*, ed. Michael D. Coogan (Oxford, UK: Oxford University Press, 2011).

11 You can access all these (and more!) in Wilhelm Schneemelcher, ed., *New Testament Apocrypha: Revised Edition of the Collection Initiated by Edgar Hennecke*, trans. R. McL. Wilson, 2 vols. (Louisville, KY: Westminster John Knox, 1992).

12 Darrell L. Bock, *Acts*, Baker Exegetical Commentary on the New Testament (Grand Rapids, MI: Baker Academic, 2007), 50.

13 Michael Green, *Thirty Years That Changed the World: The Book Acts for Today* (Grand Rapids, MI: Eerdmans, 2004), 7.

14 Gordon D. Fee and Douglas Stuart, *How to Read the Bible for All Its Worth*, 4th ed. (Grand Rapids, MI: Zondervan Academic, 2014), 118.

7   To Those with Their Backs against the Wall

1   Thurman, *Jesus and the Disinherited*, 4–5.

2   Thurman, *Jesus and the Disinherited*, xii.

3   Thurman, *Jesus and the Disinherited*, 1 (emphasis added).

4   Thurman, *Jesus and the Disinherited*, 3.

5   Thurman, *Jesus and the Disinherited*, 3.

6   Novakovic, "Jews and Samaritans," 207–16. J. Julius Scott Jr., *Jewish Backgrounds of the New Testament* (Grand Rapids, MI: Baker Academic, 2000), 197.

7   In the centuries leading up to the time of Jesus, tensions were high. The Samaritans built their own temple at Mt. Gerizim (rivaling the Jewish temple in Jerusalem). The Jews destroyed the Samaritan temple during the Maccabean period, but as we know from the Samaritan woman in John 4, the Samaritans continued to worship there. Samaritans also had their own version of the Torah, called the Samaritan Pentateuch. These rival

places of worship—with the Jews destroying the Samaritans' place of worship—and rival Scriptures were a recipe for trouble, leading to ongoing tension. Josephus, a Jewish historian in the first century, tells us that Samaritans desecrated the Jerusalem temple during Passover by scattering dead bodies in it. And violent acts went in both directions. The New Testament documents these tensions. The Samaritan woman in John 4 is shocked that Jesus would ask her for a drink because, John tells us, "Jews do not associate with Samaritans."

8   For nuances on the antagonism between Jews and Samaritans, see note 21 on Samaritans in chapter three.

9   Eric Barreto notes a similar phenomenon happening with Peter and Cornelius, which, as we'll show in chapter eight, is another instance where Peter has much to learn about God's work among those whom he would not readily share tables. Barreto ponders, "Perhaps it is Peter and his companions who leave this scene most changed. Proclamation on the move among strangers will change not only them; it will change us, too, for God has already moved ahead of us to be in their midst." See Barreto, "A Gospel on the Move," 185.

10 We regret to inform our readers that Fruitopia was discontinued in the United States in 2003—the same year Heather graduated from high school. Truly, this was the end of an era.

11 I should clarify—my mom is *very cool*. I was just too self-absorbed to recognize this as a teen. I hope I'm as cool as she is when I grow up. I may or may not say some of the things she said to me to my kids now, though I do buy them the occasional Lunchable to make up for my childhood without them.

12 Yes, cans from the pop machine only cost fifty cents. Not everything was bad about 2003, even if it was the year Fruitopia was discontinued. RIP.

13 Lamott, *Bird by Bird*, 34 (emphasis added).

14 Willie James Jennings, *Acts*, Belief: A Theological Commentary on the Bible (Louisville, KY: Westminster John Knox, 2017), 82.

15 Five times in this passage, Luke calls him "the eunuch" (8:27, 34, 36, 38, 39). It is not "the Ethiopian" who answered Philip's question or "the court official" who was baptized. It was "the eunuch."

16 We are deeply indebted to the work of New Testament scholar (and Heather's PhD supervisor) Mikeal Parsons, whose work on physiognomy, eunuchs, and Acts undergirds this section. See Mikeal C. Parsons, *Acts*, Paideia (Grand Rapids, MI: Baker Academic, 2008), 118–24; Mikeal C. Parsons, *Body and Character in Luke and Acts: The Subversion of Physiognomy in Early Christianity* (Grand Rapids, MI: Baker Academic, 2006), 17–65, and esp. 123–41.

17 Megan K. DeFranza, "Good News for Gender Minorities," in *Understanding Transgender Identities*, eds. James K. Beilby and Paul Rhodes Eddy (Grand Rapids, MI: Baker Academic, 2019), 161. See her larger chapter for how she connects the eunuch's experience to a larger theology of sexuality.

18 DeFranza explains that the priests may have voluntarily altered their own bodies

for service, though "most eunuchs were castrated against their will as babies or children when they were kidnapped or sold into slavery." See DeFranza, "Good News for Gender Minorities," 161. On ancient observations about eunuchs exhibiting different physical characteristics, see Parsons, *Body and Character in Luke and Acts*, 136.

19 Jennings, *Acts*, 83.

20 Josephus, *Antiquities* 4:290–91. The ancient satirist Lucian says a eunuch "was an ambiguous sort of creature like a crow, which cannot be reckoned either with doves or with ravens." Elsewhere he describes a eunuch as "neither man nor woman but something composite, hybrid and monstrous, alien to human nature." Lucian, *ΕΥΝΟΥΧΟΣ* [*The Eunuch*], trans. A. M. Harmon, *Loeb Classical Library* (Cambridge, MA: Harvard University Press, 1936). For a fuller survey of ancient primary literature on eunuchs, see Parsons, *Body and Character in Luke and Acts*, 133–36.

21 Parsons, *Acts*, 120.

22 Cf. Acts 3:13; 4:27; Luke 22:37.

23 For further explanation of how the eunuchs story parallels that of Isaiah's suffering servant, see Parsons, *Acts*, 121.

24 See the end of the chapter for the full quotation. Jennings puts its beautifully when he says, "Philip, while interpretating a text [Isa 53] is *performing* another text, Isaiah 56:3–5." See Jennings, *Acts*, 84 (emphasis added).

25 Paul D. Hanson, *Isaiah 40–66*, Interpretation: A Bible Commentary for Teaching and Preaching (Louisville, KY: Westminster John Knox, 2012), 195. We don't have the space to explore all the rich connections between Acts and Isaiah, but Hanson's reflections on how the vision of Isa. 56:1–8 forms a bookend with 66:18–23 are worth quoting here as they emphasize the prominence of the universal vision in Isaiah that undergirds the expansion in Acts. He writes, "Isaiah 56:1–8 is one half of a literary framework that encloses [the last portion of] Isaiah, the other half being found in 66:18–23.... In the second half of the framework, God also promises God's coming 'to gather all nations' and the return of 'all your kindred from all the nations,' from whom God would choose some to serve 'as priests and as Levites.' And, as in 56:7 God announced, 'My house shall be called a house of prayer for all peoples,' in 66:23 God says, 'All flesh shall come to worship before me'" (196).

26 For a survey of how various scholars interpret the tone of the eunuch's question about baptism, see Heather M. Gorman, "Stone-Campbell Interpretations of the Ethiopian Eunuch (Acts 8:26–40): Observations on the Last 50 Years," *Stone-Campbell Journal*, no. 23 (2020): 13. Those who think the eunuch expects a negative answer do so because of the eunuch's current exclusion from assembling with God's people per Deut. 23 as well as Luke's typical use of *kōluō* ("prevent" or "forbid") to refer to the threat of exclusion (Luke 9:45–50; 11:52; 18:15–17; Acts 10:45; 11:17).

27 Amy Hollingsworth, *The Simple Faith of Mister Rogers: Spiritual Insights from the World's Most Beloved Neighbor* (Nashville, TN: Thomas Nelson, 2005), xxii.

28 Steve Frank, "Mr. Rogers offers timeless defense of PBS funding ... in 1969," MSNBC. com, October 6, 2012, https://www.msnbc.com/the-ed-show/mr-msna21339.

29 *Won't You Be My Neighbor?*, directed by Morgan Neville (2018; United States: Focus Features), film; *A Beautiful Day in the Neighborhood*, directed by Marielle Heller (2019; United States: Sony Pictures Releasing), film.

30 Nicholas Ma, "Mr. Rogers Feels like the Hero 2018 Needs," *NBC News*, July 3, 2018, https://www.nbcnews.com/think/opinion/fred-rogers-feels-hero-2018-needs-he-wanted-people-learn-ncna888706.

31 "Motel manager pouring acid in the water when black people swam in his pool, 1964," Rare Historical Photos, accessed April 23, 2024, https://rarehistoricalphotos.com/motel-manager-pouring-acid-water-black-people-swam-pool-1964/.

32 *Mister Rogers' Neighborhood*, season 2, episode 1065, directed by David Fu-Ying Chen, aired May 9, 1969, on National Education Television.

33 Sara Kettler, "Fred Rogers Took a Stand Against Racial Inequality When He Invited a Black Character to Join Him in a Pool," Biography, June 24, 2020, https://www.biography.com/actors/mister-rogers-officer-clemmons-pool; *Mister Rogers' Neighborhood*, season 23, episode 1663, directed by Bob Walsh, aired February 23, 1993, on Family Communications, Inc.

8 Look Who's Coming to Dinner

1 Angela Duckworth, "There's No Such Thing as a Fast Learner," *Psychology Today*, November 20, 2023, https://www.psychologytoday.com/us/blog/actionable-advice-to-help-kids-thrive/202311/theres-no-such-thing-as-a-fast-learner; Kenneth R. Koedinger et al., "An Astonishing Regularity in Student Learning Rate," *Proceedings of the National Academy of Sciences* 120, no. 13 (March 28, 2023), https://doi.org/10.1073/pnas.2221311120.

2 Duckworth, "There's No Such Thing as a Fast Learner" (emphasis added).

3 This quote is attributed to George Eliot, the pen name of Mary Ann Evans, but the actual quote is this: "It's never too late to be what you might have been." However, research shows that she never said this; both quotes are falsely attributed to Eliot/Evans.

4 See Luke 5:4–11, Luke 6:12–16, and Matthew 16:16.

5 See Matthew 16:23, Matthew 8:26, and Matthew 26:52.

6 See Luke 22:54–62.

7 See John 20:3–10, 19–23.

8 See John 21:15–19.

9 Pete Enns, "Absolutely the Most Important Chapter in the Entire Bible," *The Bible For Normal People* (blog), July 13, 2012, https://thebiblefornormalpeople.com/absolutely-the-most-important-chapter-in-the-entire-bible/.

10 For "numerous Jewish sources from the Second Temple period that teach Jews ought not share meals with Gentiles or eat food prepared by them" as well as later rabbinic sources that "uniformly forbid consumption of certain foods prepared by Gentiles"

(though that differ regarding whether Jews may eat with Gentiles), see David M. Freidenreich, "Food and Table Fellowship," in *The Jewish Annotated New Testament*, eds. Levine and Brettler, 652.

[11] Michael Card, *A Fragile Stone: The Emotional Life of Simon Peter* (Downers Grove, IL: InterVarsity Press, 2006), 166.

[12] Darrell L. Bock, *Luke*, Baker Exegetical Commentary on the New Testament (Grand Rapids, MI: Baker Academic, 2007), 396.

[13] Matthew L. Skinner, *Intrusive God, Disruptive Gospel: Encountering the Divine in the Book of Acts* (Grand Rapids, MI: Brazos, 2015), 80.

[14] Lloyd John Ogilvie, *Drumbeat of Love* (Waco, TX: Word Incorporated, 1976), 145–46.

[15] Skinner, *Intrusive God, Disruptive Gospel*, 86.

9   Searching for a Theological Imagination

[1] *Jaws*, directed by Steven Spielberg (1975; United States: Universal Pictures), film; *A Few Good Men*, directed by Rob Reiner (1992; United States: Columbia Pictures), film; *Casablanca*, directed by Michael Curtiz (1942; United States: Warner Bros.), film; *Titanic*, directed by James Cameron (1997; United States: Paramount Pictures), film.

[2] *The Godfather*, directed by Francis Ford Coppola (1972; United States: Paramount Pictures), film.

[3] Barreto, "A Gospel on the Move," 175–76 (emphasis original).

[4] Luke Timothy Johnson, *Prophetic Jesus, Prophetic Church: The Challenge of Luke-Acts to Contemporary Christians* (Grand Rapids, MI: Eerdmans, 2011), 5.

[5] Here we'd like to thank Jonathan Kelley, an especially astute Johnson University student, for his feedback on thinking about Acts as improv.

[6] Barreto, "A Gospel on the Move," 176.

[7] Lawrence Hoffman, "Circumcision," in *The Jewish Annotated New Testament*, eds. Levine and Brettler, 673–74.

[8] Our thoughts on the Jerusalem Council are deeply indebted to the work of Luke Timothy Johnson, *Scripture and Discernment: Decision Making in the Church*, Rev. ed. (Nashville, TN: Abingdon, 1996).

[9] Though we don't use the terminology here, study of the Wesleyan Quadrilateral has been formative for our understanding not only of the Jerusalem Council but also of how to do theology well. The Wesleyan Quadrilateral, rooted in the work of John Wesley (though the moniker isn't his), is a theological model that relies on Scripture, tradition, reason, and experience, though different theologians understand those sources and their relative weight differently. For helpful introductions to the Wesleyan Quadrilateral, see Kevin E. Lawson, "Theological Reflection, Theological Method, and the Practice of Education Ministry: Exploring the Wesleyan Quadrilateral and Stackhouse's Tetralectic," *Christian Education Journal* 1, no. 1 (1997): 49–64; Don Thorsen, *The Wesleyan Quadrilateral: An Introduction* (Lexington, KY: Emeth Press, 2018).

[10] Yes, some of the early Christians were Pharisees, including Paul. This is important

to acknowledge because some write off the "believers who belonged to the sect of the Pharisees" (15:5) as not "real" Christians. However, even Paul, much later in his ministry in Acts, claims not "I *was* a Pharisee," but "I *am* a Pharisee, a son of Pharisees" (Acts 23:6; cf. Acts 26:5; Phil. 3:5). Their presence at the Jerusalem Council reminds us of the theological diversity that existed in the early church.

[11] Johnson notes that God is the subject of the verbs in 15:7–9 and thus the principle actor in what Peter narrates. Johnson, *Scripture and Discernment*, 102.

[12] Johnson notes of Peter: "When challenged, he does not stand on his authority as an apostle, or argue from the Scripture, for neither really covers the situation. He neither argues nor asserts. Rather, he *narrates* his own experience. This and this alone moves the others to accept and ratify his decision." See Johnson, *Scripture and Discernment*, 97.

[13] Johnson, *Scripture and Discernment*, 91–93.

[14] Johnson, *Scripture and Discernment*, 93.

[15] We want to be careful here. We are not suggesting that Peter (or other early Christians) were anti-law. In fact, Luke portrays many of the Jewish early Christians as quite the opposite. Earlier in Acts, for instance, Luke shows Peter going to the temple at one of the standard times of Jewish prayer (Acts 3:1), showing that even though he followed Jesus, he continued with many of the Jewish traditions. In Acts 10, the passage we discussed in chapter eight, Peter received his vision *when he was praying during one of the traditional times of Jewish prayer* (Acts 10:9). Later in Acts, Paul completes a Nazirite vow (Acts 18:18) and also undertakes a Jewish vow with fellow Jewish believers as evidence that he "observe[s] and guard[s] the law" (Acts 21:24). Law observance among Jewish Christians was not inherently burdensome, as both Acts and the Old Testament show; however, certain applications of that law, such as to Gentile Christians, had the potential to become an unbearable yoke, which is what Peter is pushing back against.

[16] See Acts 2:19, 22, 43; 5:12; 6:8; 7:36; 14:3. Cf. Johnson, *Scripture and Discernment*, 103.

[17] Johnson notes, "The text is confirmed by the narrative, not the narrative by the Scripture. As Peter has come to a new understanding of Jesus' words because of the gifts of the Spirit, so here the Old Testament is illuminated and interpreted by the narrative of God's activity in the present." Johnson, *Scripture and Discernment*, 105.

[18] Linda Flanagan, "How improv can open up the mind to learning in the classroom and beyond," The Hub, February 3, 2015, https://www.scartshub.com/how-improv-can-open-up-the-mind-to-learning-in-the-classroom-and-beyond.

10 The Divine Spark

[1] Andy Crouch, *Culture Making: Recovering Our Creative Calling* (Downers Grove, IL: InterVarsity Press, 2008), 90. Crouch uses the metaphor of postures (which he distinguishes from gestures) to help Christians think about different ways to engage culture. We're using the metaphor somewhat differently here but wanted to note its origin in his work.

[2] Crouch, *Culture Making*, 90.

3   Wendy VanderWal-Gritter, *Generous Spaciousness: Responding to Gay Christians in the Church* (Grand Rapids, MI: Brazos, 2014), 167–68, 129. VanderWal-Gritter uses the concept of "generous spaciousness" to help Christians think about different ways to engage conversations on sexuality. We're using the concept somewhat differently here but wanted to note its origin in her work.

4   *War Games*, written by Lawrence Lasker and Walter F. Parkes, directed by John Badham (1983; United States: MGM/UA Entertainment), film, 1:54:00.

5   This is too good not to footnote: John Benedetti, "We don't need no stinking badges!" June 8, 2007, YouTube video, 0:15, https://www.youtube.com/watch?v=VqomZQMZQCQ.

6   *Ladybird*, written and directed by Greta Gerwig (2017; United States: IAC Films and Scott Rudin Productions), film, 1:34:00.

7   Quoted in Alissa Wilkinson, "Lady Bird Is Not Just One of 2017's Best Films. It's a Beautiful, Hilarious Act of Love," *Vox*, November 2, 2017, https://www.vox.com/2017/11/2/16552860/lady-bird-review-saoirse-ronan-greta-gerwig. See Simone Pétrement, *Simone Weil: A Life* (New York, NY: Pantheon Books, 1976), 462.

8   David Brooks, *How to Know a Person: The Art of Seeing Others Deeply and Being Deeply Seen* (New York, NY: Random House, 2023), 9.

9   Growing up in Indiana (please watch the 1986 movie *Hoosiers*) and also being a passionate Liverpool Football Club fan, I (Mark) am glad to debate this particular truth with any and all.

10   David Foster Wallace, *This is Water: Some Thoughts, Delivered on a Significant Occasion, about Living a Compassionate Life* (New York, NY: Little, Brown and Company, 2009), 44.

11   Wallace, *This is Water*, 89–93.

12   Debra Hirsch, *Redeeming Sex: Naked Conversations About Sexuality and Spirituality* (Downers Grove, IL: InterVarsity Press, 2015), 172 (emphasis original).

13   Christopher J. H. Wright, *The Mission of God: Unlocking the Bible's Grand Narrative* (Downers Grove, IL: IVP Academic, 2006), 423.

14   Thomas Merton, *Conjectures of a Guilty Bystander* (Garden City, NY: Doubleday, 1966), 153–54 (emphasis added).

15   Rob Bell, "The One about Boundaries," October 15, 2017, in *The Robcast*, podcast. MP3 audio, 54:27. https://robbell.podbean.com/e/the-one-about-boundaries/.

16   We are indebted to Rob Bell for the image of birthday cake candles as a metaphor for "protecting the flame" of the image of God. See Bell, "The One about Boundaries."

17   Bell, "The One about Boundaries."

11 How to Build a Bar

1   Heineken, "Heineken – Worlds Apart, #OpenYourWorld (2017)," December 13, 2020, Marketing the Rainbow, YouTube video, 4:25, https://www.youtube.com/watch?v=z3a8MdloAAM.

2   "Heineken: Worlds Apart," Edelman, accessed April 30, 2024, https://www.edelman.com/work/heineken-worlds-apart.

3   "Heineken: Worlds Apart," Edelman.

4   Trevor Noah, "We Live in a World Where Having a Conversation is Punished," June 17, 2021, in *The Argument*, produced by Phoebe Lett, podcast, https://www.nytimes.com/2021/06/17/opinion/trevor-noah-cancel-culture.html?showTranscript=1.

5   Charles Duhigg, *Supercommunicators: How to Unlock the Secret Language of Connection* (New York, NY: Random House, 2024), 18.

6   David Brooks, "The Essential Skills for Being Human," *New York Times*, October 19, 2023, https://www.nytimes.com/2023/10/19/opinion/social-skills-connection.html.

7   Brooks, *How to Know a Person*, 12–13.

8   Many of the ideas on asking deeper questions were prompted by this podcast where Derek Thompson interviews Charles Duhigg. See Derek Thompson, "How to Have the Hardest Conversations—in Marriage, Politics, and Life," February 20, 2024, in *Plain English*, produced by Devon Baroldi, podcast, MP3 audio, 40:00, https://podcasts.apple.com/us/podcast/plain-english-with-derek-thompson/id1594471023?i=1000645985405.

9   *Ted Lasso*, season 1, episode 8, "The Diamond Dogs," written by Leann Bowen, directed by Declan Lowney, aired September 18, 2020, on Apple TV+.

10 Hugh Mackay, *Why Don't People Listen? Solving the Communication Problem* (Sydney, AU: Pan Australia, 1994), 146.

11 Dietrich Bonhoeffer, *Life Together* (London, UK: SCM, 1972), 75.

12 Thompson and Duhigg, "How to Have the Hardest Conversations."

13 Thompson and Duhigg, "How to Have the Hardest Conversations."

14 Winn Collier, *A Burning in My Bones: The Authorized Biography of Eugene Peterson, Translator of The Message* (New York, NY: Authentic Media, 2021), 274 (emphasis original).

15 Collier, *A Burning in My Bones*, 275.

16 Collier, *A Burning in My Bones*, 275.

17 Collier, *A Burning in My Bones*, 278.

18 Collier, *A Burning in My Bones*, 278.

19 Pavlovitz, *A Bigger Table*, 41.

20 Lee Camp, "The Other Fella May Be Right," No Small Endeavor, November 14, 2023, https://www.nosmallendeavor.com/lees-newsletter/posts/the-other-fella-may-be-right.

21 Camp, "The Other Fella May Be Right."

22 Vala Afshar, (@ValaAfshar), X, April 13, 2024, 02:01 p.m., https://x.com/ValaAfshar/status/1779132836202819949.

23 Barbara Brown Taylor, *Always A Guest: Speaking of Faith Far from Home* (Louisville, KY: Westminster John Knox, 2020), 36.

24 Taylor, *Always a Guest*, 36–37.

[25] We would even say that his prayer in John 17, his plea for unity, acknowledges and even presupposes disagreement and conflict. That prayer is specifically focused on Christians' relationship with other Christians. That is an important point, but we didn't want to narrow the application of generous conversations to just fellow believers. It certainly applies there, but it's not limited to that application.

[26] Taylor, *Always A Guest*, 40.

12 More Picnics

[1] Priya Parker, *The Art of Gathering: How We Meet and Why It Matters* (New York, NY: Riverhead Books, 2018), xi.

[2] Parker, *The Art of Gathering*, ix–x.

[3] Hauerwas describes well the importance of the sacraments in our gathering: "The sacraments enact the story of Jesus and, thus, form a community in his image. We could not be the church without them. For the story of Jesus is not simply one that is told; it must be enacted. The sacraments are means crucial to shaping and preparing us to tell and hear that story. Thus baptism is that rite of initiation necessary for us to become part of Jesus' death and resurrection. Through baptism we do not simply learn the story, but we become part of that story. The eucharist is the eschatological meal of God's continuing presence that makes possible a peaceable people. At that meal we become part of Christ's kingdom, as we know there that death could not contain him.... These rites, baptism and eucharist, are not just 'religious things' that Christian people do.... Through them we learn who we are." See Stanley Hauerwas, *The Peaceable Kingdom: A Primer in Christian Ethics* (Notre Dame, IN: University of Notre Dame Press, 1983), 107–8.

[4] Curt Watke, "Knox County, Tennessee, Evangelscape Profile," *Intercultural Institute for Contextual Ministry*, March 2, 2016.

[5] Michael Frost and Alan Hirsch, *The Shaping of Things to Come: Innovation and Mission for the 21st-Century Church*, Rev. ed. (Grand Rapids, MI: Baker, 2013), 68–73. We're indebted to Hirsch and Frost for this idea, which is articulated both with the "wells and fences" metaphor and through the language of bounded and centered sets, which is another common way to talk about this idea in missional literature.

[6] This idea of centered versus bounded was initially developed over thirty years ago by missiologist and anthropologist Paul Hiebert. See Paul G. Hiebert, *Anthropological Reflections on Missiological Issues* (Grand Rapids, MI: Baker Academic, 1994).

[7] Frost and Hirsch, *The Shaping of Things to Come*, 69–70 (emphasis added).

[8] *The Jungle Book*, directed by Jon Favreau (2016; United States: Walt Disney Pictures), film, 1:16:00.

[9] For data on the US, see Pew Research Center, "In U.S., Decline of Christianity Continues at Rapid Pace," Pew Research Center's Religion and Public Life Project, October 17, 2019,

https://www.pewresearch.org/religion/2019/10/17/in-u-s-decline-of-christianity-continues-at-rapid-pace/.

10   We love how Eugene Peterson's biographer Winn Collier described Peterson's accep-
      tance of such messiness: "[Eugene] was far more comfortable with ambiguity than
      most of us, and he generally assumed (a presumption many interpreted as naïve) that
      people of goodwill could honestly arrive at vastly different conclusions—and that we
      simply had to learn to live together in that awkward reality. Also, Eugene thought that
      the hardened, absolutized positions of opposing theological poles typically framed
      conversations in ways that lacked wisdom, humility, and a Spirit-inspired way forward.
      He suspected there were better questions and wider angles than our intractable skir-
      mishes." See Collier, *A Burning in My Bones,* 282.

11   Rachel Held Evans, *Searching for Sunday: Loving, Leaving, and Finding the Church*
      (Nashville, TN: Thomas Nelson, 2015), 73.

12   For more on how our proximity to others (especially others who are different from us)
      transforms us, see Michelle Ferrigno Warren, *The Power of Proximity: Moving Beyond
      Awareness to Action* (Downers Grove, IL: InterVarsity Press, 2017).

13   Brown, *Braving the Wilderness,* 120.

14   "Sitting Shiva," shiva.com, accessed May 1, 2024, https://www.shiva.com/
      learning-center/sitting-shiva.

15   We're indebted to Max Lucado's creativity in retelling this story. See Max Lucado, *In The
      Grip Of Grace* (Dallas, TX: Word Publishing, 1996), 98–104.

16   See, for example, King Solomon's killing of his own half-brother Adonijah and exiling
      Adonijah's supporter, Abiathar, when Adonijah tried to claim the throne for himself (1
      Kings 2:19–27). If a king would do this to his own family member, Saul's family had
      every reason to fear David.

17   Charles R. Swindoll, *David: A Story of Passion and Destiny* (Nashville, TN: W Publishing
      Group, 1997), 175–76.

Epilogue: A More Beautiful Way

1   Brian McLaren, "Do I Stay Christian?," July 25, 2022, in *Nomad,* podcast, 01:44:21,
      https://www.nomadpodcast.co.uk/brian-mclaren-do-i-stay-christian-n277/.

2   Franklin D. Roosevelt, "Franklin D. Roosevelt Speeches: Oglethorpe University
      Address," May 22, 1932, Pepperdine School of Public Policy, https://publicpolicy.
      pepperdine.edu/academics/research/faculty-research/new-deal/roosevelt-speeches/
      fr052232.htm (emphasis added).

3   Rob Bell describes a similar idea as it relates to the role of a pastor—that spiritual
      leaders have often been viewed as ones who give the "last word" on things. He argues
      instead that his job is rather to have the "first word," meaning he tries to start discus-
      sions, not end them. See Rob Bell, *Everything is Spiritual: Who We Are and What We're
      Doing Here* (New York, NY: St. Martin's Essentials, 2020), 123.